Disclaimer

The information included in this book is designed to provide helpful information on the subjects discussed. This book is not meant to be used to diagnose or treat any medical condition. For diagnosis or treatment of any medical problem, consult your own doctor. The author and publisher are not responsible for any specific health or allergy needs that may require medical supervision and are not liable for any damages or negative consequences from any application, action, treatment, or preparation, to anyone reading or following the information in this book. Links may change and any references included are provided for informational purposes only.

D1305681

1

Quit Drinking

Feel Good Again
The Best Ways To Be Healthy,
Happy and Motivated Without
Alcohol

By Susan Hollister
Copyright © 2017

Table of Contents

Introduction

Do you feel like you could be having a more fulfilling and enjoyable life without alcohol? Are you ready to see just how good you can be without poisoning yourself on a regular basis? If you are ready to stop drinking, but have trouble succeeding at it, you are not alone. It's extremely difficult to call a halt to indulging in alcoholic beverages. But there are incredible strategies you can utilize to start living your life in a healthier way that will allow you to feel good on a consistent basis once again!

First things first. I am **not** here to tell you that an occasional drink makes you a bad person! I am not even advocating that you stop drinking forever, although hardcore alcoholics should never touch the stuff once they do quit. A delightful "adult" beverage, as part of a meal or a festive event can be part of a perfect evening. A drink after a hard day's work can be a refreshing way to unwind. However, you probably know how that one drink can turn to many more and that is when alcohol can really start to be holding you back on your true full potential.

In the following pages you will learn all about alcohol and what it does to your brain, body emotions and your money. Then I will introduce you to some strategies that can help you slow your drinking or quit completely. You will also learn incredible strategies for keeping your body strong and your mind even stronger as you progress on your journey. So keep on reading because this is the perfect book for anyone who wants to be smarter and healthier when dealing with alcohol.

Chapter 1: My Story

The reason behind this book is to tell you about a recent discovery that has rebooted my life and might do the same with yours! As the author of multiple self-help books, I felt I had pretty much optimized every angle of my life. I know how to be successful, how to build solid good habits, how to organize both my life and my home, how to make nutritious meals, and how to make life more enjoyable. Even though I have spent much of my life focused on eating right, exercising, and living a productive and balanced mental, physical, emotional, and spiritual life, I could obviously see how alcohol was negatively impacting my life and holding me back from my true potential. I knew it was time to stop, or at least to cut back.

I tried many different strategies to curb my drinking, including a very productive time of my life when I went over 35 days without alcohol. Just one month seemed manageable to me; it sounded more like trying a diet than changing my life. I thought it would be a cinch, but it wasn't as easy as I had imagined. After many years of binge drinking once a week, the habit was more deeply ingrained in my life than I thought. When it got to point when I did this more than once a week, that is when things would really start to get bad in my life. I soon realized I would need some help to successfully kick the habit.

I doubted that I was a full-blown alcoholic in need of total abstinence, but I could sure see how my current drinking was affecting my life. The binge drinking was giving me hangovers and I would spend money on alcohol and greasy fast foods to help my stomach feel better the next day. Which, of course, leads to low energy from eating poorly, which then leads to less productivity when working, which then leads to less money earned along with other unknown possibility variables.

There was one sure way to find out if my enjoyment for alcohol was turning into something more dangerous. I would cut out all alcohol for a time and if I saw no difference, I could always go back to my previous habit. I decided to do a little research and find some tried and true methods to stop drinking on a casual basis. Stopping for about a month seemed to be the way to go so, for 30 days, no alcohol would cross my lips. Little did I know what changes were in store for me.

The first thing I noticed after committing to my alcohol fast was that I was able to fall asleep easier and stay asleep longer during the night. I also noticed my stomach healed up nicely and I enjoyed eating regular healthy meals again, the things I know I should be eating for energy and health. My skin seemed to be smoother; no more troublesome issues, and my face seemed to glow with health.

As time went on, I also discovered I was actually losing weight. Alcoholic beverages come with added calories and I wasn't consuming them anymore. My memory and my ability to think clearly improved greatly. Instead of flying off the handle when someone didn't do what I wanted, I was able to reason with them and respond more intelligently. I was able to get along better with my family and loved ones because I was more well rested, healthier, happier and mentally stronger.

In the midst of these wonderful developments, there were some negative issues that arose. I became jealous of friends who could drink freely. My cravings for that glass of wine were pretty intense at times. Depression also seemed to come upon me when I least expected it, sapping my energy.

I had decided to be up front with my friends about what I was doing. Their response was generally, "Why would you want to do that? Don't you want to have fun?" I had anticipated some reactions to my little experiment and had already planned a standard reply. Whenever someone asked why I was not joining in the alcoholic fun, I would say, "I don't feel like drinking tonight; I want a clear head." or "Maybe next time." I have found that outright refusing to drink raised a lot of questions that I just didn't want to answer.

Most people who drink think that anyone who doesn't imbibe is either boring or stuck-up. They assume that nondrinkers don't know what they are missing and are snobbish. I am guilty of thinking this myself. The interesting thing about not drinking is that you might find the friends you have been keeping are not as attractive anymore. You may need to search out some new friends who are not so attached to the bottle, but that's not a bad thing. On the other hand, you may find your friends who drink provide a bit of comic relief and good companionship. You want to do what is best for your overall wellbeing; if that means no or reduced alcohol and new friends, it's up to you to decide.

I did it! I went over a month without drinking alcohol. It wasn't easy, but I used the strategies in this book to help me get through the first 3 weeks, then just kept on going. After a month it gets much easier and that is when you truly start to notice the positive differences in how happy and healthy you are. I gladly confess it turned my entire world upside down and totally transformed my thinking. After a month, I really didn't miss my regular binge drinking sessions. I had discovered a new group of friends who were a lot of fun to be around and who had great positive attitudes. Not drinking opened my eyes to a whole new world full of delightful experiences!

Chapter 2: Alcohol, The Truly Seductive and Addictive Poison

Katherine Ketchum, in her ever-helpful text, *Beyond the Influence*, describes alcohol as "yeast poop." In short, yeast ingests sugar and spits out carbon dioxide and ethanol. When you drink the results, your body interprets the ethanol as a foreign invader (which it is; any form of alcohol kills micro-organisms) and releases an enzyme to attack it. This enzyme, alcohol dehydrogenase, defangs the ethanol by grabbing a hydrogen atom, which turns it into a substance called acetaldehyde. Acetaldehyde is even more toxic than ethanol. You can't get drunk on acetaldehyde, but if you continue to drink that delicious yeast poop, your body – which requires hours to adequately process and eliminate the poison – becomes overwhelmed. Unable to create enough of the enzyme, alcohol dehydrogenase, and unable to break down what you're drinking fast enough, increasing amounts of ethanol and related toxins are let loose to rampage throughout your body, causing damage in every quarter.

Physical Health

Unlike many diseases, which primarily affect one area, alcohol use can, over time, impact your entire body. While this is an extremely complex subject to cover in such a short space, here are a few of the physical systems affected by this poison:

Liver damage – Your liver is the largest organ in your body (after your skin) and interestingly enough, it is the most affected by drinking alcohol. There are several things that happen to your liver when you drink:

- Remember that hyper-toxic acetaldehyde that is created when your body first goes after the alcohol in your body? Guess where it is produced. Yup, your liver. Your poor liver is forced to deal with that stuff. Too much of that toxin at one time and your liver cells are damaged. If it's your habit to have a few drinks on the weekend, the alcohol can result in permanent scarring of your liver. That's what they call cirrhosis.

- Your liver uses water to do its job of detoxing your body. Guess what? Alcohol is a diuretic! What you're doing when you drink alcohol is demanding this organ to go to work on toxins, but all the while you're withholding the very substance it needs to do the work! Talk about counter-productive!

- The other way alcohol is hard on your liver is with fat. You see, your liver has the job of taking the excess glucose in your body and converting it into fat. Glucose is that wonderful sweet-tasting stuff in that latest can of beer you drank. Thanks to the sweet stuff, our liver cells can get plumped up, full of fat, especially if there's nowhere else for it to go. Over time, your liver can become stuffed like a turkey and turn into what they call a fatty liver.

Gallbladder problems – The gallbladder is not affected directly by alcohol. However, since bile is produced by your liver – and the liver is highly impacted by alcohol use – any problems your liver faces will probably impact the functioning of your gallbladder, at least eventually.

Pancreatitis is often caused by alcohol usage over time. It can be very painful – I know, from personal experience. After an excruciating bout with pancreatitis I realized my drinking was damaging my body. I had a dull aching nagging feeling constantly under my right rib cage. My general doctor couldn't tell me what it was, but after being so worried about the pain one day I actually went to the emergency room, and the doctor there knew almost immediately I had Pancreatitis. There are a variety of other factors that can aggravate pancreatitis as well, such smoking, caffeine, bad food choices, and especially alcohol! This is a nasty and painful condition you do not want!

The **brain** is also affected by alcohol. It is not impacted directly, but is affected when the liver is unable to adequately neutralize toxins. These toxins are then passed on to the brain, in turn impacting its ability to function. Some of these effects are temporary, but there is increasing evidence of long-term impact on mental functionality when the various neurotransmitters are affected. The most severe effects result in the actual shrinkage of individual brain cells, which leads the brain to become smaller within your skull. Everything from motor skills to memory is affected.

Even your **bones** are affected by alcohol consumption. Your body performs a delicate dance between osteoclasts, which break down old bone tissue and osteoblasts, which have the job of creating new bone cells. Alcohol consumption can mess up this complex choreography by accelerating the first process and slowing the latter one, so you end up with less bone density than you need to support your body.

I could go on to detail the effects on your heart, your immune system, your digestive system, etc., but I think you get the idea. Every part of your body is inter-related, so disturbing one part of it can have a major impact on the whole.

Financial Cost
I don't think you would consider a couple of drinks conducive to major decision-making. After all, pilots are not allowed to fly when under the influence, and it is dangerous and illegal to drive when you've had too much to drink. You may hope a few drinks will soften up your clients so they'll agree to your offer, but I bet you watch how much you are drinking while you're trying to clinch a major deal! You instinctively know you need to keep your wits about you and that any alcohol can take off the razor-sharp edge you need to win.

The crazy thing is, you may not think twice about alcohol's impact on your lesser decisions. How much money have you forfeited over the years, simply due to poor decisions made while drinking, even a little bit?

Even if your drinking has no other influence on your financial habits, the cost of the drink itself can add up. In an article entitled, "How Much Do Bad Habits Cost?" www.bankrate.com estimates that if you only have five drinks a week, at six dollars each you will spend more than fifteen hundred dollars a year. The site estimates that over thirty years you could have saved yourself $123,321, if you include six percent compounded interest.

If your impaired judgment under the influence results in legal problems, the cost of drinking could number in the thousands of dollars. That's before you consider the lost wages due to dealing with the impact of your drinking, costs associated with having an auto accident under the influence, or any of the healthcare costs that are incurred because your body just can't protect itself effectively anymore.

Relationships Impacted
Drinking is a funny thing. On one hand, you may find a drink helps you relax in a difficult social situation; at least that's why you take a little alcohol before you face that difficult friend or relative. Does it really help, or does it work because we *think* it will help us relax (the old placebo effect)? Perhaps it is a little of both.

On the other hand, alcohol has destroyed more relationships than it has helped. Maybe your drinking has not led to anger or violence inflicted on someone near and dear to you. Maybe you drink by yourself in the privacy of your room and don't bother anyone else. But, it's almost guaranteed that if you drink on a regular basis, alcohol has in some way impacted the way you relate to the closest people in your life. For example, it is estimated that about forty percent of all divorces are related to alcohol use by one or both spouses.

At the very least, alcohol dulls your sensitivity to the needs and feelings of other people. You are less able to empathize with people, even those you know well and with whom you are intimate. Since the alcohol in your body will reduce your thinking

15

capacity for about six hours, you may think you are picking up on a friend's unspoken signals when you're missing the real point.

Alcohol has been compared to a lover; it has a similar attraction to those who are affected by its addictive influence. Some are so enamored by alcohol they can't think of anything more important. In that sense, drinking can set itself up as a rival to other, more personal relationships. One warning sign that your relationship with alcohol is growing a little too cozy is when you find yourself turning down an evening with friends because you're more drawn to spend the evening unwinding in an easy chair with a can or a bottle in your hand. Not that there's anything wrong with the occasional drink for some people – or with that wonderful easy chair; it only raises a red flag if you prefer it consistently over time spent relaxing with friends.

Even if you doubt your drinking has any effect on your relationships or your work performance, you may want to take a break from its influence, if for no other reason than to prove to yourself that your drinking is *not* doing any harm.

How Drinking Affects Eating
It's an understatement to say that drinking alcohol interferes with a healthy diet. Alcohol stimulates cravings, especially those for fatty foods and sweets, like baked goods or chocolate, fatty foods like French fries, and other unhealthy food items. If you crave chocolate on a regular basis, like I do, you can be in a heap of trouble. At the same time, the drinker's loss of inhibition can lead to not knowing when to quit.

Conversely, drinkers sometimes forget to eat because they don't feel hungry. This combination of inconsistent and questionable nourishment only adds to the assault on the digestive system.

The Morning After
So, you had a little much to drink last night. Oh, did I speak too loudly? Sorry, I'll whisper. Your head aches and the lights hurt your eyes? Well, I can lend you my sunglasses, but I know aspirin is just what you *don't* need right now. Let me check my handy list

16

of what to do for a hangover because God knows I've had a few myself:

- The first thing I suggest is a shower. If you need to be up and moving, no matter how bad you feel, wake yourself up with a cool, not a cold, shower. If you have the luxury of time, a leisurely warm shower is just what you need. Wash away all the yucky odors, cleanse yourself of all those toxins that have leached out of your skin; wash away any less-than-pleasant memories of last night and give your body over to the gentle relaxing massage of the liquid embrace. Then come out reborn, smelling much better, and slip between the sheets for a regenerative rest.

- Is your head throbbing? Whatever you do, <u>don't</u> reach for the painkillers! When combined with alcohol, aspirin, acetaminophen, and ibuprofen can do major damage to your liver.

- I know you're groggy, but the worst thing to give you right now is an energy drink or coffee. Your real problem is dehydration because of the diuretic effects of alcohol. Any caffeine will further dehydrate you; what you really need is water, a steady slow-sipping glass of good old H2O.

- Instead of energy drinks, opt for a sports drink that contain electrolytes. This should help you rehydrate. Then go back to sipping water.

- Whatever you do, don't even think of resorting to "the hair of the dog." Come on! You don't fight poison with poison! Any more alcohol in your system will only prolong your agony, adding more time before you fully recover. What you need is time. Unfortunately, there is no way to speed up the detoxification process. It takes as long as it takes, which is at least one day for the worst of your physical symptoms. Then you need another day to recover from the poor sleep you had while coming down from the effects of the alcohol. It can take as long as a week for your mind and body to fully recover. And then, you want to start all over again? Really?

- If you truly need to be able to function in the meanwhile, a single cup of black coffee (no sugar; glucose right now is a very bad idea), sipped very slowly, and followed by a steady stream of rehydrating water, will give you the alertness you need for the moment.

- Nauseous? Stomach too upset to handle even water? Try slow sips of mineral water. The bubbles will help settle your stomach and the water will work to reverse the dehydration that caused the nausea. Switch back to regular water when you can "stomach" it again.

- Remember when you were sick as a kid? What did your mother feed you to help settle your stomach? Well, your stomach is just as sick now, so start it off easy with some dry toast or saltine crackers. Of course, you'll want to wash it down with some plain water. You'll actually want to sip water throughout the day. It'll take quite a bit of water before your body is able to recover from the dehydration you've inflicted on it.

- Eat an egg, but not a fried egg. Anything greasy will be hard for your stomach to handle right now. Eggs contain cysteine, an enzyme your body needs to break down that nasty acetaldehyde generated while your liver is slaving away to break down the alcohol in your system. The best source of cysteine is anything soy-related, but eggs are usually more accessible. Other high-quality sources are beef or any kind of meat, sunflower seeds, and oats.

- I know you're feeling guilty right about now for all the unhealthy stuff you ate last night, but now is not the time to start a health food kick. Salads and energy bars are not what your body needs at the moment. It needs to restock its supply of some key nutrients. In addition to cysteine-laced foods, eat a banana to help replace the potassium you've lost and an orange or other citrus fruit to start building up your vitamin C.

- Likewise, you may feel guilty about mistreating your body, so you think a trip to the gym is in order. You think you'll sweat it off. That simply is a bad idea because you are already badly dehydrated. Any physical exertion now will cause you to sweat, that much is correct, but when you sweat you lose water, right? That's even more dehydration, the opposite of what your body needs right now. Save your guilt-driven workout for a few days from now.

- In the meantime, take an early evening amble through the woods. (Remember your sunglasses.) The light will be less harsh then and the trees will shield you from any excessive glare. Breathe in deeply to fill your lungs with fresh air and expel any toxins lurking inside. As the fog in your mind clears, let your gaze leisurely move around you, taking your time to let your eyes focus gently on the plants and any animals that enter your field of vision.

  Mosey for as long or as short a time as you want. The purpose of this stroll is to gently re-enter the land of the living, preparing your mind and body for a fresh start tomorrow, following a full night's rest.

Life Lost
"...alcoholism...is fatal and characterized by dependence, obsession, compulsion, and loss of control. It is always headed toward insanity and death."

– Harry Haroutunian, MD, in *Being Sober*

The blunt truth is that alcohol, as a poison, can be fatally toxic. Here are a few well-known individuals whose lives were cut short by alcohol. The world is the poorer for their absence. May they rest in peace.

- Amy Winehouse – Died of alcohol poisoning, July 23, 2011 at age 27.

- Mickey Mantle - Died of liver cancer (partly due to excessive drinking), August 13, 1995 at the age of 63.

- John Bonham – Died after a bout of binge drinking, asphyxiated on his own vomit, September 25, 1980 at age 32.

- Elaine Rivera – Died from liver cirrhosis, October 26, 2013 at the age of 54.

- Alexander Godunov – Started out as a ballet dancer so accomplished that when he jumped, he seemed to be suspended in air. He defected to the US from the USSR and became an actor. He died of acute alcoholism, May 18, 1995 at the age of 45.

- Billie Holliday – Jazz singer, stopped drinking for a time and then started again. She died of drug and alcohol-related causes on July 17, 1959 at the age of 44.

- W. C. Fields – Died December 25, 1946 of a stomach hemorrhage brought on by alcohol abuse; he was 66 years old.

- Richard Burton – was nominated for seven Academy awards but never won. He was 59 when cirrhosis of the liver and kidneys took him.

- Ryan Dunn – star of the television show "Jackass" drove his car while intoxicated and was killed along with his passenger. His alcohol level was two times the legal limit and he was 34 years old.

- Jack Kerouac – writer, poet, screenwriter, and artist died at 47 from a hemorrhage caused by drinking.

- Hank Williams – popular country singer and song writer, died at 30 from an alcohol-induced hemorrhage.

- Errol Flynn – the dashing original Robin Hood dropped dead at age 50. The autopsy revealed heart disease and cirrhosis.

- John Barrymore – actor and grandfather of Drew Barrymore, died at 60 when he collapsed while a guest on a radio show. He slipped into a coma and died. The cause was alcohol.

- William Holden was *the* leading man in movies of the 50's. He was drunk when he fell, hit his head on a table, and died. His body was found four days later.

Chapter 3: The Benefits of Being Alcohol-Free

Great things can happen when you're not drinking. Since you've stayed with me this far, I assume you're at least slightly curious about how living without alcohol for, say, thirty days can help you. While everybody is different, here are some common changes that occur:

Physical

- Lost weight – This is the most noted side-effect of living without alcohol. It is accompanied by a sense of feeling healthy.

- Fitness – Many people report feeling fit, lean, and energized. You might be tempted to go out and indulge in a new wardrobe that shows off your new physique.

- Reduced fatty liver – Alcohol is the primary cause of fatty liver, a condition indicated by a lack of energy and a general feeling of discomfort in the belly. Fortunately, this can be reversed before it leads to more serious issues. Limiting or eliminating alcohol intake, along with a healthy, varied diet with plenty of fresh fruits and vegetables, can do a lot to allow your liver to repair itself. Controlling your cholesterol, maintaining a healthy weight, and sustaining normal blood sugar levels, all contribute to a healthy liver.

- Almost everyone remarks about how much smoother their skin feels and how it glows, now that their body is flushed free of alcohol-related toxins.

Emotional

- After a couple of weeks without alcohol, individuals report feeling happier.

- Some people report feeling like they are now really living, instead of just existing from day to day.

- Many report feeling "more enthusiastic" about life in general, and their own life, in specific; they describe their previous existence as being "average" or "mediocre."

- Another common remark is that individuals feel they have more control over their emotions.

Relational

People who have ceased drinking are surprised to learn that social situations can be just as enjoyable without the aid of alcohol. Here are some of their observations:

- It is possible to be introduced to someone without handing them a drink. Sometimes it is just better to walk over and start talking to them.

- I can still "party like a rock star with little or no alcohol." (James Swanwick).

- I am still an interesting person without alcohol.

- I am starting to understand who I am and I am able to let others see the real me.

Financial

- Alcohol is not cheap. Even if you just drink on weekends, a decision to hold off on the alcohol will guarantee you some financial savings.

- You can also save money on secondary costs, such as taxi fare to get home safely after drinking.

- Your grocery bill may benefit as well, if you eat junk food or feed your cravings after drinking alcohol.

- If you miss work occasionally after drinking, taking a short hiatus from alcohol will likely increase your income.

- Likewise, your productivity both at work and in other pursuits can boost your income and further your accomplishments.

They're Famous…And Alcohol-Free

There are plenty of people in the world who've either never drunk actively, have decided they're either better off without alcohol altogether, or have chosen to dial back on their imbibing of spirits. Here are a few who are rather well known:

- Bradley Cooper – Cooper realized early on that his involvement in alcohol and drugs was harming his life. When newly sober, he found himself surprised that other people found him interesting just as he was, without the booze, and has since embraced the challenge of discovering himself, alcohol-free.

- Blake Lively – This actress loves to cook with alcohol but has no interest in drinking it. She is part of a growing list of celebrities who choose to live an alcohol-free lifestyle.

- Kristin Davis – Davis started drinking in her teens and would have persisted, but for her love of acting. In her twenties, she realized she could have one but not both, so decided alcohol would have to go. She has been a teetotaler ever since.

- Blake Anderson – Well-known in running circles, this super-healthy Ironman owes the start of his success to an addiction to alcohol. Anderson tended bar around the world until he decided to quit drinking. Now he runs, swims, and bikes, instead. Blake claims he traded one addiction for another, but this seems to have done him no harm. He still passes up temptation regularly as he still tends bar, all the while completing one physical challenge after another.

- Kim Cattrall – Despite appearing in advertisements for Bacardi, Kim Cattrall reportedly doesn't drink much at all, because alcohol gives her a headache.

- Tyra Banks lives a life without alcohol as a matter of course. She says she has only had a sip once in her life and has no interest in drinking.

- Jennifer Hudson surprised an interviewer by stating she had never in her life had a drink. This seems to be her normal lifestyle.

- James Franco has portrayed characters that imbibe but he is drug-and alcohol-free. My guess is that he just doesn't have the time to waste on getting drunk.

- Stephen King – The famous novelist was confronted by friends and family with the effects of his drinking in the late 1980s. He got help and has been sober ever since.

Chapter 4: Burning Your Ships

Well, we've covered both sides of the bottle. In the previous chapters we've described both what happens when you drink, and what can happen when you abstain from alcohol. This is the part where I ask you what you're going to do about all this information. Of course, I have no inkling about your own circumstances. Maybe you're confident that your drinking is not harming your life. Perhaps you are fully aware that your drinking is getting in between you and where you want to be. Or maybe you don't yet know what you think.

Wherever you are, I'm not here to browbeat you into swearing off booze for life, but I *am* going to present an opportunity to stop for just one month, just to clarify matters.

It's Time To Commit
The first time I ever went rappelling, was in the Smokey Mountains. We set up at the top of a sheer drop-off. From our vantage point we could see for miles above the tops of the trees. It was a gorgeous view. Before long I was harnessed up and ready to go. That's when my instructor spoke the words that have shaped my life, "It's time to commit." He was asking me to lean back over the edge, trust my life to a thin length of rope, and begin to step down that rock face. It's risky. It's a matter of backing into the unknown. Yet, I would never know if I could do this unless I took that first step and committed.

That's what I'm asking you to do now. You can stand here looking at the scenery and thinking about everything you've read, but until you commit you'll never make any progress, you'll neither know the terror of facing the unknown nor the thrill of conquering new territory. Nobody can do this for you. I have plenty of help to offer you while you're on the way, but until you commit, nothing in the rest of this book will do you any good.

Oh, and this isn't something you just "try"; you gain no benefit by just trying it out, with the idea that you can bail out of this adventure whenever you like. No, to get any benefit from this experiment, you must make a firm commitment to live without alcohol for a full month, no exceptions. After all, thirty days isn't the end of your life; it's just a measly handful of weeks. After that time, you can choose what you want to do going forward.

Today Is The First Day

So, did you decide to opt in? Great! (Even if you are still here and haven't decided yet, there's nothing wrong in reading about what you'll experience when you *do* take the plunge.)

There's no time like the present to act on your commitment. Mark today as the first day of your 30 days of alcohol-free living:

- Jot down a list of the ten things that will help you most in your quest to live without alcohol for a month. Work these into your action plan and come back to them whenever you are feeling "iffy" about the whole affair.

- Select a few friends who you know will be supportive and tell them you are taking a month-long hiatus from alcohol. You might want to arrange to have one or two of them "on-call" when you need them.

- Put a great big star on today's date in your calendar to mark this as the first day of your alcohol-free challenge.

- Start a journal to record this experiment in alcohol-free living. Use whatever format is comfortable to you. You can write in a hardbound blank book, grab a spiral notebook, or open a new file on your computer. Whatever you do, mark this as a special log of how you fulfilled your commitment. Record your thoughts, your feelings, including your fears and difficulties. Keep track of any changes you notice in both mind and body.

- Next, decide what will be your go-to beverage of choice whenever you are faced with an opportunity to drink. For myself, I have chosen a refreshing cold glass of water with a twist of lime. It's easily available anywhere. Some people resort to flavored or fizzy water; you might opt for a refreshing glass of ice tea.

No Retreat

From time immemorial, leaders have chosen to consolidate the commitment of their troops by cutting off all avenues for retreat. One of the most well-known is a conqueror of many lands named Alexander. With his soldiers freshly landed on the Persian shore, he chose to burn the ships they had used to make the Mediterranean crossing. All chances for retreat destroyed, the soldiers had no choice but to fight their way inland and take the country that lay before them. If they went home again, they would be sailing Persian ships!

Now that you've made the commitment to stop drinking for a month, it's time to figuratively burn your ships, making it easier for you press forward into this new lifestyle. It's time to rid your house of all alcohol:

- If you can, pour out all the alcohol in the house. Down the drain it goes; you don't want ANY that you can get your hands on while you are at home.

- If you live with someone else who is not part of this challenge, either cover their bottles with plain paper or ask them to keep alcohol out of your sight for the duration of the commitment.

- Move anything that reminds you of drinking away from eye level. If you have a collection of beer cans on a shelf in your media room, pack them away for the month.

- If you can't bear to pour out all your alcohol, give it away.

- If you can't bear to give it away, ask a trusted friend to keep your booze in safekeeping away from your residence for the duration of the challenge.

- Opt for alcohol-free mouthwash and get rid of any cough medicines that have alcohol in them. You might not be tempted by these things during your abstinence, but then again you might, so it's best not to have them around.

- Do whatever it takes to remove all opportunities for drinking from your home.

One individual who took the challenge remarked:

[Your drinking] is a canoe on the Pacific. It may keep you afloat for a while, but at some point, you're bound to be overturned...I don't know about you, but I'm sinking my canoe in favor of a bigger, better vessel. And even if I find myself resurrected each morning in the hull of that tiny boat, I'll commit it to sinking again.

– *Coming Clean* by Seth Haines

Chapter 5: Dangers to Watch Out For

It is very important that you prepare yourself for your alcohol fast. Not too many people can quit cold-turkey and it is wise to be informed and have a plan. We will present an action plan later in this book, but first, let's see what you might expect to happen

Danger Signs Of Alcohol Detoxification

You may think you are not addicted to alcohol because you only drink on weekends or have a drink once or twice a day. Your body may have other ideas about this and it is very important that you pay attention to what your body is doing during your alcohol fast. Alcohol withdrawal symptoms range from the moderate to life-threateningly severe; they can accelerate quickly with possibly deadly consequences.

Literally, alcohol withdrawal has the potential to kill you. Everyone is different; while one individual can get away with a drink a day and not be physically dependant on alcohol, another person might not be so lucky. This is why you must really pay attention to what your body is telling you for six to 48 hours after you take your last drink.

I would suggest that you do not do this alone. Have someone you trust nearby for this critical period and educate them with what might occur and how to handle it.

Social Drinker Vs. Addiction

I always thought myself to be a social drinker and assumed I could take it or leave it. Addiction is insidious because it sneaks up on you. That is why this month-long fast from alcohol is important. If you truly are just a social drinker, you should experience few to no effects from alcohol detox. However, if you have become addicted to alcohol, the effects of withdrawing "cold turkey" will be much more dramatic. Symptoms start out mild but grow in intensity, eventually making you want to give up and take a drink, just to make the symptoms stop. This is a huge red flag that most probably indicates addiction.

I have an uncle who can drink and never show any effects from it. He seems the same whether or not he is drinking; I do not think I have ever seen him drunk. My uncle is a hit-and-miss drinker; he doesn't drink every day, not even every weekend. He may drink on a holiday or a special occasion. I would consider him a social drinker who, if he decided to stop drinking for a month, would have few to no problems. His body chemistry is such that alcohol does not bother him much.

Now my mother, his sister, on the other hand, will become quite tipsy on just one drink. She also only drinks on occasion, simply because she knows her tolerance is terrible. She is a social drinker, but restricts her drinking to sipping a single drink at an event. My grandfather, however, drank every day for years. Although he never became tipsy, when he had to abstain from drinking for medical reasons, it was sheer hell going through detox.

Because each person responds to alcohol differently, it is very difficult for you to figure out for yourself whether you are a social drinker or you are addicted to alcohol. Here are a few scenarios:

Let's say your kids, aged three and five years old, are playing and little Bobby gets cranky, as do most three-year olds when they don't get their own way or need a nap. Bobby starts crying because his brother has a favorite toy and won't give it to him. A fight ensues and you have to break it up and send the kids to their respective rooms. You want a drink to calm your nerves. The kids are quiet in their rooms. You don't usually drink when things get chaotic, it is just this day. You grab the vodka from under the cupboard and pour just a little into a glass and drink it. That is it, you don't drink anything else and you don't do this every time the kids get into a fight. If you fit into this scenario, you probably don't have a problem with alcohol. It would only be a problem if your spouse came home night after night to find you draped over the bed in a drunken stupor.

In this second example, your boss accuses you of not doing your job well and forgetting to submit an important report that was due several days ago. You know you didn't do what you were supposed to do and you blame it on just about anything you can think of, including other co-workers. At lunch, you find yourself at the local bar having a drink to calm your nerves instead of eating a nutritious meal. This is the third time this week that you visited the bar over the lunch hour, just to get a drink to help you cope with being treated unfairly at work. If you identify with this situation, you have a problem with drinking. You are using alcohol as a crutch and blaming everyone but yourself for your inadequacies.

Although the two scenarios should both send up red flags, the mom who only occasionally imbibes to calm her nerves is probably not addicted. She only *wants* a drink and she may or may not actually take one. The person with problems at work who has been to the bar for the past four lunch hours definitely has problems.

The difference here is between *needing* and *wanting* a drink. If you want a drink, but can take it or leave it, you probably do not have an addiction. If you need a drink after lunch every day because of work pressures, you should pay attention to your behavior, because you are probably addicted.

It is important to note that any type of alcohol can be addictive. The guy who drinks 10 beers a night is just as addicted as the lady who guzzles down three to four glasses of wine in an evening or the man who goes to the bar for eight shots of whiskey. It doesn't matter what you drink. You can get just as addicted to alcohol using fancy ice wine as you can to cheap Strawberry Hill.

Detox Symptoms To Watch
As stated before, you may not experience any withdrawal symptoms at all from alcohol. Your symptoms may be extremely light and inconsequential. This would lead me to believe that you truly are a social drinker who does not have an addiction.

My dad knew firsthand about addiction. His father was an alcoholic, so because of that, plus the fact that a few of his brothers were also hooked on alcohol, he avoided it. I think he only had one or two drinks a year at New Years Eve and Christmas Eve. If he decided he wanted to swear off alcohol entirely, he would have suffered very little.

His sister had a few beers every weekend. Once she started gaining weight because of it, she decided to stop. She had very mild symptoms and the detox process did not bother her much. Another brother was a heavy drinker and because of legal issues was forced into recovery. He experienced withdrawal symptoms so severe that he had to be hospitalized. So, you can see, the extent of alcohol's effects on you will depend on how much you drink as well as your metabolism.

Withdrawal

Withdrawal symptoms usually begin to appear about six to eight hours after you have taken your last drink, but they can surface as early as two hours later. Withdrawal symptoms are at their peak between 24 and 48 hours after your last drink and will start to dissipate in five to seven days. The following are symptoms you need to watch for:

- Cravings for a drink can get pretty intense even after a few hours of not having anything. Try to distract yourself from those cravings as best you can and drink soft drinks or water with some citrus added. Ice tea is refreshing, too.

- Tremors in hands and legs – Also called delirium tremens or DTs, these tremors can be mild to serious. Most people do experience DTs from alcohol withdrawal, but it is seldom severe. They can be lethal however, so it is nothing to fool around with. During DTs you may feel confused, irritable, angry, depressed, or anxious and you may experience nightmares. You may have a headache, nausea and vomiting, and you might sweat profusely. This last is one of the first symptoms of withdrawal to appear.

33

- Falls are frequent when detoxing, mostly because of the destabilizing nature of DTs. That is another reason you'll want someone around to keep an eye on you during this time.

- Dehydration is a common problem during withdrawal, mostly because it is very hard for the stomach to stand even water. However, you must try to stay hydrated. Water is your best option, but it might be hard to swallow. Fizzy water can sometimes relieve the upset stomach, at least a little. If you suspect dehydration is serious and you can't stop vomiting, it is best to go to an emergency room. You have not failed if you need medical help, you just need help. Do not be too proud to get that help if you need it. It is better to get help than to be dead.

- Hallucinations might appear at around 12 to 24 hours into the withdrawal. This is another reason you want someone to be with you during detoxification. The hallucinations can be very mild. You may find yourself standing in front of the refrigerator and can't remember how you got there or why you are there. You might also have some nasty hallucinations and feel your life is in danger. Severe hallucinations are nothing to fool with. They are another valid reason to head for the emergency room.

- Seizures are a possibility from 24 to 48 hours into detoxification. About two to three percent of individuals who go through detox experience some form of seizure, often brought on by dehydration. Seizures may involve convulsions and falling, but they may also consist of just staring into space or being unable to respond to stimulus. If you go into convulsions your friend should call for emergency help. The best thing a helper can do if you are convulsing is to roll you onto your side and stay with you, preventing you from banging into anything that could hurt you.

Go To The Hospital

If you have any of the following symptoms, be safe and get to the hospital:

- Temperature above 101 degrees Fahrenheit

- Pulse rate of 115 or more – download a pulse rate monitor to your smart phone. They work pretty accurately.

- Systolic blood pressure of 170 or higher.

- Severe dehydration – not being able to keep anything down for eight hours or more.

- Convulsive seizures.

- Uncontrollable hallucinations

Do not take the chance of harm from any of the above.

I am not trying to frighten you out of your month of abstinence, but I would be remiss if I did not let you know what is possible during an alcohol detox. I certainly don't want any harm to come to any of my readers.

In most cases, your symptoms will not be severe; mine weren't that bad. I experienced DTs for a while but they were tolerable. I had no hallucinations, seizures, high temperature, or racing heart problems. My craving for a drink was pretty intense, but I had someone there with me who distracted me from it most of the time.

The experience of detoxing is uncomfortable to be sure, but remember that nothing good ever comes cheap. You can do this; you'll be glad later, if not now.

Do your homework so nothing will be a surprise. This includes exploring methods of sobriety. There are many from which to choose and you can try one or do a combination of several. We will explore some of these methods in the chapters that follow. This will give you some help in forming your own action plan for drinking cessation.

It is important you understand what could happen. You may be one of the lucky ones who have no problems at all, but then again, your body could react to the detoxification process in any number of ways. It's extremely important that you watch for the warning signs and get help immediately if necessary. Detox symptoms can escalate quickly, with deadly results. Don't become a statistic. You want to be able to enjoy your friends, your family, and your life for a long time.

Chapter 6: The Best All-Natural Methods

I am a firm proponent of using natural methods to enhance my physical, mental, emotional, and spiritual health. The practices suggested in this chapter fall into one of two general categories: the *restoring* of areas that have been stressed, poisoned, or damaged by alcohol, including the things we've been relying on alcohol to fix – and the *exchanging* of old ways of thinking and acting – replacing old habits with new ones, replacing old ways of thinking about ourselves with a fresh self-image, etc. Not drinking anymore will open up a whole world of change in your life, and change can involve some fear, so let's deal with that first.

How To Handle Change

You may encounter a variety of feelings connected with this sudden change of not drinking:

- You may **enthusiastically embrace it**. Some people naturally thrive on change. If you are like this, be glad. Your only danger is a tendency to embrace change without fully considering and preparing for the challenges that will appear. As we move through this book, we will talk more about what you can expect to encounter in the next month, and I will suggest different ways you can choose to deal with them.

- **Resistance** is another possible attitude toward change. Sometimes we have an instinctive knee-jerk reaction against a proposed change. If this is you, you have already overcome the greatest difficulty by choosing the no-alcohol challenge in spite of your inner resistance! Kudos, friend.

  A response of resistance is usually caused by something deep within that we may or may not fully understand. A little further on, I will give you the tools to discern where this reaction originates and to figure out what to do about it.

37

- With or without resistance, you may be feeling **fear**. Fear is a natural response when facing the unknown. The unknown *is* change by its very nature, so some fear is to be expected. In addition, you may have a fear of something that alcohol has been masking up to now. What seems like a shrinking back may be your mind telling you that it doesn't know how to face situation X without alcohol.

  Since you will not have that option for the near future, I can help you look your fears in the face and answer them. Ultimately, fear is nothing to be afraid of; it's a bully that cannot answer to the strategies I will give you a little later in this book.

- You also may be getting a case of **cold feet** about now. "What have I gotten myself into?" you may be wondering. Whatever you are feeling right now, I recommend you accept it as valid. Embrace your emotions as part of your experience right now but understand that they are not *who* you are. Whatever you are feeling right now has no power to unmake you. *You* are the one who makes your decisions, not your feelings. *You* are the one who acts on those decisions and experiences their results, not your feelings.

When you are able to untangle and detach yourself from your feelings a little bit, you will be able to look at your fear or your anger a little more objectively and start to get down to why you are feeling this way. Only when you understand this "why" will you be able to find a true resolution.

Some of the following suggestions might seem silly, but you won't know if they work unless you try them. You might find they are really good distractions that work like a charm.

Relax And De-Stress

Laughter
The wise man who said laughter is good medicine was right. There is scientific evidence that laughter reduces pain levels,

stimulates those feel-good endorphins, and helps both mind and body relax. Thirty days without alcohol, especially if you are in the habit of drinking regularly, will tax your mind to create new ways to deal with life's realities. In short, your brain will get tired. You owe it to your mind to give it a break every day.

We each have a different sense of humor. What has me rolling on the floor with laughter may leave you in the cold and vice versa. All I can do from a practical standpoint is offer a variety of sources that can serve as a springboard for your fertile imagination:

- Cartoons — go back to those old Disney cartoons and watch the cat chase the mouse, chortle gleefully as the roadrunner eludes the coyote, and the canary once again gets the best of the cat. It's simple, almost childish humor to be sure, but I bet you can't watch without a smile cracking your face. One of the good things about enjoying cartoons if you have kids, is that you can participate with them. Ask them to choose their favorite cartoons and watch with them. Some modern cartoons are really quite funny. I find myself giggling at Gravity Falls or Bob's Burgers. Archer is another or try Rick and Morty. All of these can be found on Netflix or Hulu just; don't let little kids watch the last two.

- Comedy Films — Here tastes diverge wildly. I belly laugh over *The Princess Bride* and Danny Kaye's *Court Jester*, but you may laugh yourself silly over *A Christmas Story*, which I can't stand. The best movies are the ones you can watch over and over again and they still make you giggle…or guffaw, or snort…however you express yourself. Other great comedy movies that the whole family will enjoy are *Young Frankenstein, Blazing Saddles, Ghostbusters, Spaceballs, Police Academy, Robin Hood – Men in Tights,* and *Elf*.

- Kittens and puppies — You're either loving or hating me at this point. If you enjoy the antics of animals, there are plenty of YouTube videos out there to enjoy, if you don't already receive a steady stream of them from your friends. Look up pigs, baby goats, and bunnies, too.

- Children – Any children: your children, a friend's children, or children at play in the park. Little kids, especially, can be hilarious to watch as they explore their world. If you add in puppies or kittens to the mix, well…

- Bloopers – These are also available in abundance on YouTube, or you can bring up an episode of "America's Funniest Home Videos."

- Pranks – If your humor has a sadistic streak, you can always watch TruTV or search for pranks on YouTube. Or you can invent your own.

- Hidden Camera – Okay, most pranks use hidden cameras, but this genre also explores the quirks of human nature in ways that go far beyond pranks. It began with "Candid Camera" and continues with "Girls Behaving Badly," "Scare Tactics", and "Impractical Jokers." Some of the wackiest hidden camera shows for some reason come from England.

- British Comedy – Some people get it, others don't, but British comedy has a style all its own.

- Comic books – The first comic books were either about superheroes or were the equivalent of what we know today as cartoons. Today a wide variety of comic books are available, from slapstick to what I call "intelligent" humor. Whatever makes you laugh. Be careful though, because there are some very dark comic books out there that will certainly *not* make you laugh and won't help you at all.

- The Funny Papers – Does anybody still read newsprint today? If you get the daily newspaper, whether the hold-in-your-hands kind or the digital version, skip the news of madness and mayhem and go straight for the good stuff: the comic strips. They're always more fun if you can share them with someone for a good laugh. If you find one comic strip that tickles your funny bone excessively, check the bookstores for more of the same or pull up the strip's website.

- Stand-up Comedians – You can attend live shows or find plenty on YouTube videos to watch. A lot of comedians produce their own podcasts. While there are too many wonderful standup comedians to mention, a few of the performers who really crack me up are Dylan Moran, Nate Bargatze, and Ross Noble.

Meditation

There are quite a few different ways you can approach meditation. The West tends to look at it from a cognitive angle, while the East will appear to most westerners as vague, intuitive, or mystical. Different religious traditions have a variety of ways to incorporate meditation into their practices. Before you dismiss this section as a bunch of hooey, please be aware that our culture tends to have little respect for things we cannot measure or explain; for many people, meditation is just that. However, it has been known to provide deep healing. Please suspend your disbelief long enough to look at these brief descriptions of common meditative practices; you may actually find something relatable that you can use to your benefit.

There is a growing body of evidence to show that meditation, especially mindfulness techniques, reduces impulsivity, regulates the emotions, and reduces feelings of distress.

- Mindfulness – This strategy is pretty much what it says: the conscious awareness – and control – of your mind. While it may smack of eastern philosophy, and indeed it is a hallmark of Buddhist meditation, this is the direct opposite of what you do when you have a beer or a glass

41

of wine. Mindfulness is a practice that can serve as a direct antidote to alcohol.

Our fast-paced, high-stress lifestyle seems to demand that we focus our thoughts everywhere at once, all the time. Alcohol provides a loosening of the reins, letting the mind relax. The practice of mindfulness does the same thing, but without any negative side-effects.

William Alexander, a recovered alcoholic and practitioner of Zen Buddhism, remarks that drinking is "the disease of living elsewhere." He promotes mindfulness meditation as a way to restore ourselves to ourselves, teaching us to be fully present. The emphasis is on being, over doing. Alexander's book, *Ordinary Recovery*, provides practical exercises in everyday mindfulness.

For a clear description of mindfulness practices, I recommend watching the YouTube video, "60 Minutes Special on Mindfulness – Anderson Cooper" presented by Palouse Mindfulness.

- Breathing – You will find this plays a major part of mindfulness practices, as well many therapeutic strategies. Breathing exercises are key to controlling the flight or fight reflex that can easily arise in the midst of our jam-packed days. Breathing exercises are readily available online, but I offer here a simple strategy you can utilize almost any place, any time:

To start with, find a quiet place. Sit or stand still in a relaxed but alert posture. Concentrate on your breathing. Breathe in slowly for a count of five. Hold your breath for another five counts and exhale slowly for five counts. Repeat this process until you are calm and your mind has stopped bouncing around (or until the phone rings, again). This exercise distracts the brain and disconnects it for a moment, just long enough for you to take control, calm yourself, and then go on with your day, more fully present.

Use this technique any time during your month-long challenge to help you handle anxiety, fear, or cravings.

- Meditating on words – Throughout the ages, Jewish and Christian faithful have practiced this type of meditation. The Hebrew word for meditate is "hagah," which literally means to growl, to muse, or to mutter. If you've seen pictures of Jews before the Wailing Wall, you'll know that they literally speak the words of their scriptures aloud. There is something about hearing yourself say a sentence that gets into your mind from a different angle. You can repeat a single sentence several times, emphasizing a different word each time, and drawing deeper meaning each time you encounter the text. This type of meditation actively engages your mind and your heart as they work together to help you learn: about yourself, about God, about the world around you, and your place in the universe.

  Speaking aloud can also be a powerful tool for internalizing affirmations, or statements of purpose. These are short sentences you have consciously chosen to describe your ideal life. The more often you repeat them aloud to yourself, the more deeply they sink into your psyche and influence every part of your being, even your subconscious.

- Tai Chi and Qigong – While these practices are forms of meditation in motion, I have chosen to put them in the "exercise" category, so take a look further down for more information.

Socializing
What energizes you? They say there are two types of people, those who are energized by being around other people, and those who are energized by withdrawing from people to a silent place. Sometimes I find myself fading from too much "people time" and need to go off alone to recover myself. Most of the time,

however, a lively party full of people who are being their own glorious selves rejuvenates me and increases my joy.

If socializing is where you do your serious drinking, you don't have to become a hermit for 30 days. I know from experience that it is indeed possible to have a great time without alcohol, even if you're in the midst of a bunch of people holding glasses. You can still be the life of the party; you may find it even more enjoyable because you will remember every lovely moment with clarity the next day. The secret is to go prepared:

- For the first ten days, try to surround yourself with people who won't make an issue of you not drinking. You'll be learning to manage your own cravings during this time, so you don't need the input of friends who may side with your cravings instead of with your choice.

- Plan ahead of time what you will use as your go-to beverage of choice. My go-to beverage is a glass of ice water with a twist of lime. It doesn't look suspiciously nonalcoholic and is easy to order wherever I go.

- You also need to plan in advance what you will say on the occasion that somebody notices you are not drinking your "usual." If someone catches on that you're toting around a non-alcoholic beverage and asks why, the ladies can lie and say they are pregnant, but lying isn't advisable. Often, it's enough to say that you've chosen to take a short break from drinking.

  If you are pressed, it also helps to decide on a statement that will – hopefully stop them from pestering you further. A few snappy comebacks are: "It looks like you're drinking enough for both of us" or "I make a big enough fool of myself *without* drinking" or even, "I'm afraid, I'd be even more boring if I *did* drink." Your plan should include an exit strategy for getting away if you are being hard pressed and start to crack under the pressure.

- Find a non-judgmental non-drinking buddy. Whether you're facing a casual dinner out with the boss, a holiday party, or just a night out with friends, having an ally within the group who knows about your hiatus from alcohol can be a big help. Just knowing that somebody present knows about your commitment can be enough to strengthen your will against any offered drinks or inner cravings. Your friend can also help you extricate yourself from sticky situations.

- I suggest you agree beforehand on a cue or key phrase as a sign that you want to exit the scene. There's nothing wrong with extracting yourself from the party before it ends. Especially in the first couple weeks, you may well find the strain of socializing around alcohol rather exhausting. Now is the time to treat yourself with a little gentleness. Don't try to tough it out. When your mind, body, or emotions tell you that you've had enough, step away and give yourself a break. Oh, and plan your exit excuse before you even hit the party. It can be something as simple as saying you have an early morning ahead and need to get some rest. You may not need to use it, but you never know when it'll come in handy. That old go-to statement, "I feel a migraine coming on," is also a good way to get out of a situation.

- Get to know the new you. Prepare to discover new things about yourself. Even if your drinking has only been occasional, you may discover new likes you never paid attention to before. There may well be a delightful person waiting inside, as you emerge from the dampening effects of alcohol. You may find yourself drawn to people and events that held no interest before; in short, you may find your life a whole lot more interesting.

Sometimes, especially when people have been self-medicating with alcohol in order to dull the pain of a loss, a trauma, or an emotion that is too much, emergence from alcohol means facing a difficult reality. However, once the thing that drove you to drink in the first place is dealt with, you may uncover a fresh love for life. In addition, you may find a whole well of energy. You may find a sense of humor you never knew you had, or realize you have a whole host of admirable qualities that have been untapped for years.

Sleep

Adequate and quality sleep is so important to restoring your body, mind, and emotions that I have written an entire book on the subject! While you may wish to refer directly to the eBook, here are a few tips that may help you:

Follow an evening countdown as follows:

- Five hours before bedtime, eat your last meal. This gives your body time to do the heavy labor part of digestion before it's time to let your body rest. This doesn't mean you can't have a small snack before bed if you want one; just keep it light.

- Four hours before bedtime, drink your last caffeine of the day. Taper off drinking all liquids as well; you don't need multiple trips to the bathroom to disrupt your night's sleep.

- Three hours before bedtime, smoke your last cigarette of the day. Nicotine is a stimulant that can interfere with deep, restorative sleep.

- Two hours before bedtime, prepare what you can for tomorrow. This will set you up for a low-stress start to your day. Select and lay out your clothes. If you take your lunch or snacks to work, prepare them and place them either together in the refrigerator or in another convenient location. Put in the same spot anything you will need to take with you in the morning. Find your keys and place them in an area that is easily accessible. I cannot tell you how much tension is added to my day when I can't find my keys in the morning.

- One hour before bedtime you should start to ramp down your level of activity, lowering the volume and the intensity of what you do, see, and hear. Put away everything work- or study-related. If you take a walk, make it a leisurely one. During this time, you should begin to wean yourself off all your electronics. If you want to read, hold a real book in your hand and choose content that is light and refreshing (no *Texas Chainsaw Massacre*, please).

- Thirty minutes before bedtime, begin your going-to-bed ritual. Use this time to prepare both your mind and your body for sleep. You want to establish a routine you follow consistently. This will minimize your stress by following a familiar practice nightly. It can also have a powerful psychological effect; your mind and body will eventually interpret this ritual as its cue to prepare for sleep, making it easier for you to drift off to dreamland. While everyone's routine will differ, here are a few practices you might consider:

  o Take a leisurely bath to relax your body and let the stresses of the day wash off.

  o Review the positive events of the day with gratefulness.

  o Practice yoga or meditation.

  o Pray and rest in God's presence.

  o Read more of that relaxing book.

Biofeedback
This is the classic reality of mind over matter. It is absolutely possible for you to change what we usually think of as automatic

functions: heart rate, blood pressure, digestion, etc. You can even learn to change your brain waves, with training. Even something as simple as stepping outside and looking out into nature can lower your blood pressure. This can be most useful if your cravings lead to anxiety.

While you will see the most thorough results at the hands of a professional with training in providing biofeedback or neurobiofeedback, it is possible to accomplish some changes yourself.

Hypnosis – Hypnosis has proved useful in helping individuals get over a wide range of problem behaviors, including drinking. If you are worried about your ability to stop drinking successfully for 30 days, you might want to check out the available YouTube hypnosis videos.

Physically Detox

Herbal Methods
For centuries we've known various plants can heal and restore our bodies. Here are some herbs that may be able to heal damage and ease your body's transition to an alcohol-free way of living. Go to your local health food store for capsules or tea for the following:

- **Milk thistle** helps the liver recover from damage and generate new liver tissue. Recent research has documented its effectiveness in stimulating recovery from alcoholic hepatitis, fatty liver, and cirrhosis.

- **Dandelion** is well-known as a blood purifying agent. As such, it can help with liver recovery, clearing the skin, and boosting the metabolism.

- **Kudzu** helps the liver process alcohol in your system and protects it from damage. It can also treat headaches and reduce your cravings for alcohol.

- **Echinacea** builds up your body's immune system and can help your body fight infections.

- **Passionflower** can help your digestive system return to normal and can also help you get to sleep.

- **Valerian root** can also induce sleep. It is known for its mild sedative properties, so is also recommended when you are having difficulty relaxing.

- **Cayenne pepper** can help reduce cravings for alcohol as it boosts the appetite.

Acupuncture

The use of acupuncture can assist you by lessening your cravings. It can also help with any underlying stresses and anxieties that "drove you to drink" in the first place. While acupuncture cannot change the cause of your anxiety or fear, it can help reduce your feelings of fear and anxiety, freeing you to face and successfully deal with their sources.

Massage

The mere chance of being on the receiving end of a massage would be sufficient to keep me away from drinking! In my book, a massage is the best way to treat your body. Never mind that a soothing massage can work deep into your tissues to break free the toxins that have built up inside. Never mind that the reinvigorating kneading of your muscles can relax them and cleanse away the stresses you feel too weak to bear. All you need to know is that a massage is really good for you, all of yourself, body, mind, and spirit. By giving yourself over to the kind ministrations of a skilled masseuse (or masseur), you are breathing fresh life into your soul. Oh, and while you're at it, a massage can help reduce your cravings for alcohol and lessen any fear or anxiety you may be carrying around.

Reinvigorate

Exercise

Your body was engineered to function by alternating times of activity with times of rest. However, our urban lives often keep us from moving around. We sit when we work. We sit in a car as we wend our way between work and home. We sit before a television at home. Even a stimulating computer game usually stimulates no muscles beyond our thumbs!

Because our culture tends to encourage us to be sedentary, a commitment to regular physical activity is all the more important. Generally, any physical activity that your body can tolerate is helpful. The only caution is that during your detox period you should stay away from strenuous exercise; it can cause dehydration and place too much stress on your heart during this time.

We Need Exercise:
1. To keep our circulation, well, circulating. All parts of our bodies need the nourishment of fresh liquids and nutrients in order to grow and to flush out dead stuff and toxins that have nothing to offer us. Our circulation is stimulated by physical motion.

2. To strengthen our bones and muscles. Our bones respond to stress placed on them by building new bone tissue and, when we are older, by slowing the loss of bone density. Your body builds up the parts you use the most; That's why it's important to regularly move each part of your body by walking, running, lifting, swimming, climbing, etc. It probably goes without saying, but the only way to keep your bones and muscles strong is to use them daily. Do this by regularly performing load-bearing exercises. These could be as simple as climbing stairs several times a day or devoting time to tromping around the grassy hills (if you have any) in your neighborhood.

3. To strengthen our hearts. The heart, as you probably know, is a muscle. When it beats on its own it is constantly contracting and releasing. At least *this* part of

your body is exercising, whether you choose to exercise it, or not. However, to keep your heart functioning at peak capacity, it must be exercised at near its peak performance level, on a regular basis.

The general consensus is that you need to do some activity that will get your heart beating fast enough that you feel warm and are slightly out of breath. That is, you want to exert yourself to the extent that you can still carry on a conversation while you're moving. They say you should do this every day for a total of thirty minutes. These thirty minutes don't have to be experienced all in one fell swoop, either; you can split them into several shorter sessions and achieve the same cardio-strengthening results.

"They" also say that a couple times each week you should replace this moderate activity with more strenuous activity, where you can still talk but you find it difficult to carry on a long conversation as you move. This, too, can be split up into several sessions scattered throughout the day.

4. To keep our bodies flexible. The phrase "bend so you don't break" is true of our physical bodies. The longer we live in our increasingly sedentary culture, the easier it is to minimize our movements, until we have lost much of our ability to bend as well as much of our sense of balance. Stretching counteracts this tendency.

While I perform a few gentle stretches when I first wake up, stretching is generally frowned upon until your body is somewhat loosened up. Do some easy walking, stair climbing, or bicycling until you feel warm and your heart is pumping just a little faster than usual. Only then should you gently stretch out your neck, your torso, your legs, your arms, and your shoulders. When you feel gentle tension on a muscle, hold it for a few seconds, then gently stretch just a hair farther before releasing. Oh, and don't bounce. Bouncing when you stretch can lead to injury, damaging the very muscles you're trying to build. The best time to stretch is after you have exercised and your body is still warmed up.

Tai Chi

This is the original slow-mo exercise, but don't underestimate it. Tai Chi has benefits for strength, flexibility, circulation, and especially balance. It incorporates a form of mindfulness meditation along with carefully prescribed motions, designed to unite the body as a whole. When I am practicing Tai Chi, I find I think clearly, I am more aware of both myself and my surroundings, and my movements are much more coordinated in everyday life.

Positive Reinforcement

While your 30-day alcohol fast is one of the kindest ways you can treat yourself, your mind and body may not get the message, at least not initially. Since your body won't thank you in words, it's important that you thank and appreciate yourself for what you are doing. Anything you can do to reward yourself will help get the message across to the rest of you.

Link these positive reinforcements to accomplishments connected to your 30-day challenge. You might want to reward yourself after a particularly difficult day, or mark the end of a week of nondrinking with a special treat. Think of things you really enjoy and add them to your list of possible rewards. Here are a few possibilities to get you started:

- Treat yourself to a long soak in a tub; candles, soothing music, and bubble bath are optional.

- If you're a people person, have friends over for a make-your-own-pizza night. Ask each person to contribute a pizza topping while you provide the dough and the sauce.

- Give yourself free time. Grant yourself thirty minutes to do anything you want to do. If your life is jam-packed, this can be a valuable reprieve.

- Give yourself time for a haircut, or gift yourself with a manicure and/or pedicure. This is time for you to relax and enjoy a little pampering.

- Try something new. Especially if you love exploring, go to a different part of town to do your shopping, go to a museum or concert, someplace you don't normally visit. If you like to walk, find a new park to explore. Test-drive your dream car, just for grins. Go to a shop and try on hats, just for fun. Watch a kids' movie. Go fly a kite.

- Buy yourself a bouquet (and have it delivered to your office with a love note). Or buy yourself an ice cream cone. Whatever makes you feel special.

- My favorite idea is to put one of those little metallic stars on the calendar for each day that goes by without drinking. It may sound trite, but as the stars fill each block in the calendar without a break, you can feel proud that you truly are making progress. It can be a real confidence booster. You have taken on a task that is difficult and you are actually succeeding!

Replace

Habits
We all know about habits. The experts say it takes about 21 days of consistent repetition to establish a habit.

What you are doing over the next thirty days is exploring possible activities that can serve as alternatives to drinking alcohol. Eventually, instead of thinking of things in terms of alternatives to drinking, these new activities can become valuable in their own right.

Drinking Triggers

In the first two weeks of your non-alcohol challenge, you will be especially aware of things that have triggered drinking in the past. You can plan ahead for these triggers, either removing or avoiding them. If a trigger can't be removed from your life, I recommend you decide beforehand what you can use as an alternative activity.

An alternative activity can be something as simple as texting a friend or calling someone you enjoy talking with. You can focus on reading a book or any other pleasurable activity that will displace that trigger from your attention. It is a distraction that you need and a positive one.

When you're bored – You'll probably notice you have a lot of spare time on your hands when you stop drinking. What can you do with all that time? Lest your boredom turn to drinking, you'll want a list of things you enjoy doing or have always wanted to try.

Stave Off Boredom With:

- A movie night, at home or at the cinema; don't forget the popcorn and soda! To save money, you can always check movies out from your local library.

- Computer games; keep an alternative beverage (see below) close at hand.

- An online class; what have you always wanted to learn about? There are many free classes from which to choose; you can also use some of the money you will save by not drinking to take a credited coarse.

- A visit with someone you haven't seen for a while, either by phone or in person. Visit your favorite aunt and uncle or opt to go see grandma at the nursing home. Your older family members will appreciate the visit and it will make you feel good too.

- A game of solitaire, a jigsaw puzzle, a Sudoku, or a crossword puzzle

How To Chill Out With Friends:
- A game of basketball, football baseball, or golf (putt-putt is *my* game).

- Watching a game of basketball, football, baseball...or golf.

- A card game with (nondrinking) friends.

- Have a cookout.

- Have a picnic potluck, all the more interesting with spouses and kids.

- Have a dinner with friends where they bring the ingredients and you do a mass cook-off.

- Bring your own alternative beverages with you.

- Bring a friend for a hike in the park or woods.

- Take the family or friends to an art gallery or a museum and see what you can discover.

Alternative Beverages

There are plenty of tasty nonalcoholic beverages you can find in stores. Many come in glass bottles that appear real enough that few people will catch on that you aren't drinking the hard stuff. If you want a healthy beverage you can buy smoothies or iced coffee in your local grocery store. For additional varieties of alternative beverages, visit a health food store.

When you're at home there are a host of tasty beverages you can easily whip up. If you're used to having a glass in your hand when you unwind after work, fill your favorite glass with one of these:

Smoothie: Put the following in a blender and whip it up into a frothy smoothie: 1 cup unsweetened frozen peaches, ¼ teaspoon vanilla, 1 tablespoon honey, 1/8 teaspoon ground cinnamon, pinch of ground ginger and nutmeg, ½ cup low fat milk and ½ cup plain yogurt. Yum!

Spritzer: Mix a favorite fruit juice with sparkling water and a little ice. My favorite is cranberry juice.

Lemonade: Pour it into your favorite glass straight or mix it with iced tea.

Iced tea: With or without lemon. Try sweetening it with honey or stevia if you want.

Chai tea: Who doesn't love the delicious comfort-food aroma of chai? Drink it cold with ice or hot, to warm your innards and make you feel good.

Positive Affirmations
Do you have fears of failing? Do you doubt you have it in you to succeed in the 30-day no-alcohol challenge? Give yourself the best chance of succeeding by working to counteract any negative thoughts or doubtful fears. The best way to start reframing your mind is to envision yourself as succeeding by speaking positive affirmations to yourself. They really do help you believe in yourself and your God-given capabilities.

Affirmations are phrases you speak to yourself in order to reframe your underlying attitudes. Some examples of positive affirmations are:

- I deserve to be happy.

- I am strong and full of self-control.

- I am worthy of love.

- I see the good in all people and situations.

- I am grateful and glad to be alive.

- I am generous, giving, and caring.

- I act quickly and decisively.

- I will grow today by following good habits, eating healthy food, and pursuing positive relationships.

- I am super-creative and perform flawlessly.

I encourage you to create your own affirmations that pertain to your plans for the next thirty days. Write them down on cards you can slip into a pocket, billfold, or purse. Post a copy up where you can see them when you're getting ready in the morning. Speak them out loud, at least 20 times when you wake up and before you go to sleep at night. During the day, repeat them as well. My habit has been to pick an activity I do several times a day and use it as my cue to speak my affirmations to myself. I've used bathroom breaks as my cue. Other people have used whenever they get in their car as a trigger. You can even use your cravings as a cue to repeat your affirmations.

They say you've had years to build habits of negative self-talk; the experts recommend repeating your affirmations as much as 200 times each day. Don't kill yourself at it, just do what you can. I've spoken positive affirmations to myself for several years now and can attest that they have truly helped me redirect my thinking toward a more positive outlook on life. They really helped to boost my self-confidence during my month of abstinence.

Chapter 7: Getting The Support You Need

Video Support

There are many online resources that can encourage you, distract you from cravings, and help reframe your thinking. The more you can fill your mind with positive messages that reinforce your choice to go alcohol-free for 30 days, the better. While it's important to give your mind adequate down-time to process all the changes you're throwing at it, video support – in moderation – can be just what you need. Here are a few YouTube videos you may find helpful:

- "Five Lessons We Learned Quitting Alcohol For 30 Days" by Make More Marbles

- "SOBER Inspirational Documentary" by Gareth Bowler

- "How Do I Relax Without Drinking Alcohol?" by AlcoholMastery TV

- "Alcoholism: 10 Tips to Quit Drinking Alcohol" by StopDrinkingAlcohol.com

- "How To Stop Alcohol Cravings" by AlcoholMastery TV

Good Movies for Inspiration

Recovery from alcoholism seems to be an inspirational topic for many movies and these will actually give you a supportive boost.

Probably my favorite rehab movie is *28 Days* with Gwen Cummings and Sandra Bullock. In this movie, the main character doesn't think she has a problem but because of a drunken binge, she is court ordered into a 28-day program. This film presents a comic view of life in a rehab facility; it makes you laugh, but it also makes you think.

My Name is Bill W is a movie about one of the founders of Alcoholics Anonymous, tracing the history of how he came to be one of the most important names in alcohol rehab. The film describes Bill Wilson's addiction and how he transformed his life through abstinence.

Denzel Washington stars in the movie *Flight* about a pilot who has a drug and alcohol problem. When something goes wrong during a flight, he is able to save the passengers on his plane, but the investigation reveals he was under the influence when he was flying. The movie reveals some interesting assumptions people have about addiction.

Clean and Sober is a Michael Keaton movie. Keaton plays a real estate agent who goes through alcohol counseling and treatment. This movie gives you a good idea of what treatment is all about.

If you have a significant other who is not affected by alcohol, you both need to watch *When a Man Loves a Woman*. In this movie, the husband is a pilot who is often away from home. He does not see his wife drinking frequently and only realizes she needs help after a dangerous situation arises. The movie lets you view the treatment process through the addict's eyes and also from the partner's point of view.

Will Farrell plays a man who relapses on alcohol and loses his job and his wife, in *Everything Must Go*. He tries to start over by selling everything in a yard sale and ends up meeting a neighbor who becomes important to his new, sober life.

Key Organizations
The most helpful organizations are those that provide a supportive community of nondrinking individuals. They can fill in the gaps where friends or family are unable to be there to support you. Here are some of the main organizations that can help you …

- Alcoholics Anonymous (AA) – The most well-known and frequently-utilized response to alcoholism, AA's twelve steps to recovery and its support group meetings are often the first resort of the drinker. The organization began in 1935, so it has a long tradition of helping individuals who drink.

Wherever you are, you can likely find an AA meeting to attend, with people who are accepting and supportive. You can locate AA meetings anywhere in the world by going to the AA website or calling the mental health offices in your area. You will likely find many meetings per day from which to choose.

Most meetings are held in churches or public buildings and are run by regular nonprofessionals. The program is built around the belief in a higher power, one that you may identify in any way that you want. If you would prefer a secular view to recovery, the next organization may be more to your liking.

- The Secular Organization for Sobriety (SOS) at www.sossobriety.org offers a secular alternative to Alcoholics Anonymous. It is a non-profit and meetings are also run by regular people, not health care professionals. Meetings are similar to AA meetings, but without any mention of relying on God. You can find meetings on their website; if there are no meetings available in your area, they do have the option to attend web-based meetings.

- Celebrate Recovery is a Christian-based twelve step program. It consists of face-to-face meetings provided in a church setting, usually led by a trained facilitator who is often the pastor of the church. It is built around twelve steps that relate to verses in the Bible and eight principles based on the Beatitudes.

- If you prefer to stay away from faith-based programs, check out SMART Recovery's four-step cognitive therapy program. The four steps consist of building motivation, coping with urges, problem solving, and finding lifestyle balance. Based on the latest scientific discoveries, the organization equips individuals to live a balanced life apart from addictive substances. SMART stands for "Self Management and Recovery Training." You can learn more at www.smartrecovery.org. The website does offer web-based meetings and a treasure trove of resources.

- Women For Sobriety (WFS), established by Dr. Jean Kirkpatrick, helps women attain sobriety and sustain their recovery. This non-profit organization has been around for about 30 years and deals with the unique problems women face in trying to maintain sobriety. The WFS New Life Program consists of 13 acceptance statements that help women grow spiritually and emotionally.

- The National Institute of Alcohol Abuse and Alcoholism, or NIAAA, offers many resources to recovering individuals. This organization has done a great deal of research on how alcohol can affect you and provides funding for research that includes genetic links, treatment effectiveness, and addiction in general.

- The National Council on Alcoholism and Drug Dependence, Inc., or NCADD, is another organization with a wealth of information on alcohol and drug addictions. Around 70 years old, the organization also provides connectivity to local treatment facilities. Its founder, Marty Mann, was one of the first members of AA and one of the first to recognize alcoholism as a disease. Her sponsor was Bill Wilson, one of the founders of Alcoholics Anonymous . NCADD has been instrumental in organizing employee assistance programs for many businesses and labor unions.

Other Helpful Resources

James Stanwick is an entrepreneur, a former ESPN anchor on Sports Center, the host of the James Stanwick Show, an author, and the creator of the 30-day No Alcohol Challenge. His paid program equips you with everything you need in order to go for a month without alcohol. As part of the program, James invites you to join a closed Facebook community. I really benefitted from the support offered by the people in this online group. The program also includes daily email podcasts. The daily dose of encouragement I received from these podcasts made a huge difference in my life.

- Check Your Drinking (CYD) has an 18-question form that will help you find out how your drinking issues rank in comparison to others. It is completely anonymous, but gives you the option to print the survey so you can carry it with you to discuss with your doctor, counselor, or other professional advisor.

- Your First Steps to Change provides you with questions and answers related to drinking and is a website provided by Cambridge Health Alliance, affiliated with Harvard Medical School. This site gives you a bunch of great information and makes you really think about your problem drinking issues.

- The Alcohol Help Center is a web presence that offers tools to keep sobriety going in your life. There are discussions, handbooks, assessment tools, suggestions on how to create goals, help in planning your recovery, reward systems, availability to a coach, access to motivational emails, and much more. You can choose to register or not and everything is completely anonymous.

- Online recovery forums, like Recovery.org, are also available. These sites provide discussion, encouragement, and advice, all of it confidential. The support is very good at this site.

In the next chapter, we will explore different methods of achieving sobriety that range from going to support meetings to attending a special clinic for recovery and participation in various psychological methods of treatment.

Chapter 8: The Best Modern Methods

12-Step Programs

According to its website (www.aa.org), Alcoholics Anonymous, the original 12-step program, is "an international fellowship of men and women who have had a drinking problem." It is "nonprofessional, self-supporting, multiracial, apolitical, and available almost everywhere." The organization, established in 1935 (just after the repeal of Prohibition), is most well-known for its twelve-steps, which have been useful in helping individuals take responsibility for their own drinking choices and the consequences, while charting a new, alcohol-free life.

It is possible to work the 12 steps without participating in formal rehabilitation program, but many rehab facilities use the 12 steps as a key component of their programs. Working the 12 steps, whether by yourself or under supervision, can definitely benefit you and help you stay sober.

When you attend an AA meeting, you will be greeted by people just like you. They may be in recovery from excessive drinking, and will be, like you, in abstinence. Some are old-timers who have sustained their sobriety for decades; others are trying to abstain but are struggling. In the meetings, you will hear testimonials from those who have been where you are and from others who have been much worse off. These people come from all walks of life, ranging from executives to factory workers, all the way from the retail clerk to the stay-at-home mom.

You will learn all about the 12 steps to sobriety through the meetings. If you start working through each step, you may find it a little easier to achieve sustained sobriety yourself. The big plus is that you will probably make some of the best friends in your life in the process.

The 12 steps center around recognizing you have a problem (sometimes that is harder than you might imagine), surrendering to a higher power for assistance, performing self-analysis of your problem, attempting reconciliation with people who may have been harmed by your actions, and carrying the message of the 12 steps to others who may need it. Most members have sponsors within the organization. Sponsors are individuals who have been members for a while and are very familiar with the steps. They give advice and come alongside to help you when the urge to drink is strongest.

AA's 12-step program is Christian-based, but other faiths use the 12 steps in their quest for recovery, as well. There are Jewish, Muslim, Buddhist, and Hindu 12-step programs; all rely on these steps as an aid to recovery, often citing wisdom from their holy writings in their support.

Results from the most recent studies reveal that the 12 steps are slightly more successful than other traditional methods for alcohol recovery in use today. According to researcher Joseph Nowinski PhD, "being immersed in a 12-step program of recovery…leads to categorical commitment, and it is that commitment that seems most predictive of recovery." (*If You Work It, It Works*)

Certified Addiction Therapy Programs
12-step programs are run by peers; they are not officially certified programs of recovery. Here are some methods most often utilized by certified alcohol recovery clinics that are supervised by professionals. Unlike peer support groups, these programs would be facilitated by a trained and licensed counselor or therapist.

Motivational Enhancement Therapy (MET)
MET works on the principle that you will only successfully quit drinking on your own when your motivation is strong enough. The focus is on fueling the individual's motivation and the therapy consists of only four sessions. Seeking out a counselor who can provide this therapy at the start of your no-alcohol challenge may be useful if you feel you need stronger motivation to carry you through. It will not harm you and may increase the ease of your

experience. Because the duration is so short, MET focuses on stirring up your desire to stop drinking.

The first session is the most intense. An assessment is completed and you will be instructed in the process of building a personal action plan for change. The next chapter in this book will show you how to create this plan for yourself, but it might be helpful to work through this process with a certified professional who can offer insights you may have overlooked. Other sessions may include developing coping strategies, and learning strategies to stop drinking. Along the way, your therapist will provide wonderful encouragement, the one thing that can carry you through, when your "won't power" is at its weakest.

Motivational enhancement therapy is used in a variety of situations, but it seems to be most effective with those who want freedom from alcohol. It causes you as a drinker to take a good look at yourself; it motivates you to want to change, and equips you to go after that change. The program takes a good look at your background: health issues, family, what you want to happen in various social settings, and more. The counselors are trained to be empathetic to your problem and are often themselves in the later stages of recovery. The program aids you in discovering the difference between what your life is like now and what you want it to be like. It then helps you to set goals and objectives that will help you reach that ideal. The therapists are helpful and sympathetic and continue to provide ongoing motivation. Used along with cognitive behavioral therapy, this method can be highly effective.

Cognitive Behavioral Therapy (CBT)
This works on the theory that you started drinking because you are lacking in specific skills needed to cope with something in your life. The focus of this counseling style is the identification of coping skills that aren't working for you, followed by the development of alternative strategies that *do* work.

We talked earlier about the common ways we respond to change. At that point I mentioned that sometimes we have a knee-jerk opposition to change, opposition that is all out of proportion to the size of the change we're facing. If this describes your first reaction to the idea of going without alcohol for thirty days, then you might benefit from this type of counseling. It can help you get to the bottom of your resistance and discover more appropriate solutions to the issues that have been driving you to drink. If you are pretty confident that you drink in order to handle certain situations, cognitive behavioral therapy may be just what you need to navigate your way toward a response that does not involve alcohol.

What you *think* you will surely do in a certain situation, dictates what you *actually* do and how you feel in that situation. If you think you are going to have a bad day, you most likely will. If you think you will want to drink after having a fight with your significant other, you will probably take a drink. With cognitive behavioral therapy, you learn how to rethink the attitudes behind your actions. You are given the opportunity to transform destructive, negative thoughts into positive ones in order to change your assumptions, and thus your actions. You un-learn negative thinking, replacing it with alternatives that are positive and life-affirming.

Other things that cognitive behavioral therapy can help you understand are:

- The world does not look at you and see your failures. In fact, most people won't even notice them.

- Most people accept that you aren't necessarily the cause of any failure you may have experienced.

- Things you know to be true, may not hold true in every situation

- Almost nothing is black and white; there are many different shades and variations along the way.

- If you have a fight with your significant other, you can learn to think and respond differently. You can learn how to talk things out, and gain skills to smooth down those ruffled feathers and re-establish a relationship of trust.

I particularly like cognitive behavioral therapy because it includes exercises and assignments that seem to bring the techniques more into focus for me. Journaling is one of those assignments that more than anything else helped me to see the ways in which my drinking was damaging my relationships. It also helped me learn to deal with the difficult people in my life. My avoidance of these difficult relationships triggered my increased drinking. I was stressed out because I couldn't control what they thought of me; neither could I control their actions. It helped me to understand that their opinions belonged to them, not me; once that soaked into my mind, my attitude changed toward them and now we get along much better.

Contingency Management And Motivational Incentives

These methods involve incentives to reinforce positive behavior. It is usually used with motivational enhancement therapy or cognitive behavioral therapy to support abstinence between counseling sessions. Your therapist will offer vouchers for a treat when an alcohol screening comes back negative. This works particularly well for adolescents, but it can be equally effective for adults, especially those with limited emotional development. The treats may be food related, they could consist of a movie or concert ticket, T-shirts, or other rewards. There is some troublesome discussion about this method, however, because in some circles, it is thought to promote a positive association with gambling.

In-House Treatment Options

If you find you need something a little more organized and you need to be away from the influences that surround you at home, you may want to look into options that place you in a totally new, controlled, environment.

Retreat Centers

Retreat centers range from the simple to the expansive – and expensive. They offer the individual a monitored setting that is isolated from the stresses of normal life, where you can safely recover from the physical effects of alcohol and get a fresh start at life.

Alcohol Treatment Clinics And Centers

These exist in almost every county of every state. Many are run by the mental health board of the state and provide both housing and counseling in a safe environment. Just like retreat centers, they range from the bare-bones treatment – a twin bed in a double- or triple-occupancy room with a nightstand and three meals a day – to some rather opulent centers that provide king-sized beds, heated swimming pools, concerts, and other amenities. If you lack the money to spend on a fancy center, you will receive the same adequacy of treatment if you attend something simpler. In most cases, alcohol and drug addictions are treated in the same community.

Treatment may consist of the following:

- Detoxification/Withdrawal Management – The detoxification process (or detox, for short) usually lasts anywhere from three to seven days in length. Medications may be given to reduce the most severe withdrawal symptoms. A 2014 Substance Abuse and Mental Health Services Administration report stated that about 80 percent of the clinics in the US used these medications to help patients cope with their detox symptoms. Medications that alleviate cravings may be administered even after an individual leaves the facility. Patients are gradually weaned off these medications as their treatment continues. .

- Detoxification is an inpatient program, but while there you will usually receive care that goes beyond mere physical detox monitoring. During this time, you may be introduced to one of the different therapy methods we described previously. You will experience group and individual counseling, you'll be set up for case management, and may be introduced to community-based peer organizations like Alcoholics Anonymous.

- The next stage of rehabilitation involves the outpatient program. Some outpatient programs provide sober housing for patients, either on the premises of offsite, with transportation provided to the inpatient location. Some outpatient programs allow you to live at home; these leave it up to you to get to the center for groups sessions and treatment.

  Outpatient programs vary widely and often include a variety of therapeutic methods. Some outpatient programs include therapy in the form of therapy animals, art therapy, or music therapy. If you live on the premises, treatment will take place every day, but when you live off-campus, treatment can consist of three to four times a week.

- Aftercare is less intense. It is designed to encourage abstinence and to provide a little boost to your daily life. It will often begin with weekly meetings to touch base with your counselors, but aftercare is designed to taper off gradually until you are able to function successfully on your own.

Some of the less intense treatment phases can coincide with your work schedule so you can continue to work and participate in work activities and family functions.

With all these methods from which to choose and all the resources provided both in this book in your community, you should be able to pick and choose what you personally need. I am not saying that everyone reading this book requires therapy or should get into counseling. I am only letting you know what is available and what to expect if you realize that you need outside help to strengthen your resolve.

Chapter 9: Your Personal Action Plan

Warning: If you start your month-long abstinence from alcohol and suddenly start shaking, find yourself filled with anxious panic or deeply depressed, these are signs that your body is throwing a life-threatening hissy fit about you depriving it of alcohol. You need to **seek professional medical attention immediately**.

Likewise, you should not take this challenge without first checking with your doctor, especially if you are under doctor's care for *any* ongoing condition.

The following summarize my suggestions for implementing your own month-long no-alcohol challenge. Feel free to personalize your own plan, choosing from the suggestions throughout this book, as well as any others you encounter that will fit your needs. Whatever plan you use, stick with it. May you succeed beyond your wildest dreams!

The First Week – Be Kind
This is the week to practice being kind to yourself. You and your body are going through a lot of changes simultaneously, so it's important you start things out with an open mind, ready to receive whatever is thrown at you. You may become grumpy and easily ticked off. You may find yourself thinking thoughts and feeling emotions that are unfamiliar, or unusually intense. That's okay. Just as your body is detoxing from alcohol, so your soul may want to be purged. At the same time, be aware that some of your thoughts and feelings are just your body throwing a fit because it wants alcohol. This is the week to take everything with a massive grain of salt. Remind yourself that things will simmer down after a while. Even if you have to put up with a few days of misery, things *will* get better.

Cravings
You can expect cravings to arise as soon your body realizes it is not getting its usual dose of sugary intoxicant, so be prepared for

the onslaught. While the cravings could crop up off and on for months, they will be most intense in these first two weeks.

There are two basic approaches to managing your cravings – distraction and riding them out. While, ultimately, you will have to tough out your cravings, it is important to do so while mindful of what is going on in your psyche.

If there are **unresolved issues** that have contributed to your drinking, these must be consciously acknowledged, even if you are not in a position to deal with them at the moment. And I do *not* recommend tackling them during this first week. You already have enough on your plate, nursing yourself through this difficult time of getting toxins out of your system.

When these issues arise, acknowledge that you have used alcohol in the past to help you with this. Then reaffirm to yourself, "I have chosen to take a total break from alcohol for 30 days." Don't let these triggers get off scot-free, however. When one rears its ugly head, write it down in a special part of your journal, labeled "Stuff to Deal With Later" and tell it, in your best Arnold Schwarzenegger voice, "I'll be back!" Then turn your mind toward something else.

This week, especially, is going to be an exercise of mind over matter. Your cravings will come at you from any and every angle. You may feel like they're swarming around and you are spending all your time batting them away, but this is normal.

Surf Your Cravings
One useful technique for riding out your cravings is called "**urge surfing**." It consists of visualizing an oncoming craving as a wave that starts small, then swells in intensity before subsiding again. You "ride" the wave on a surfboard that consists of your breathing. You keep your breaths steady, long, and slow, as the desire rises and falls. The idea is that you are retraining your mind not to respond with anxiety when insistent cravings arise. The theory is that the cravings will eventually grow less frequent and less intense over time. This is the opposite of fighting an urge;

instead of battling the craving head-on, you simply observe it without responding in any way other than just riding it out, surfing it.

Distraction Tactics

This is the Week of the Cravings. If you choose the tactic of distraction, your strategy will consist of turning away from your cravings, and consciously choosing to focus on pretty much anything else. Here are a few things you can do to **counter your cravings**:

- Remind yourself of your "why" for this 30 days of nondrinking. Keep the description handy on your phone or somewhere else you can easily access.

- Use your imagination to envision what your life will be like when you are free from cravings for alcohol. Paint a colorful mental picture of your perfect day.

- Replay in your mind the latest movie or TV show you watched, trying to remember the entire plot.

- Pay attention to what you can see around you. Start naming off everything that is in your field of vision, in great detail, using the format, "I see _____."

- If you like to dance, use every craving as an opportunity to break into your favorite dance step, celebrating your choice of continuing to live alcohol-free.

- Sing a favorite song, trying to remember all the words.

- If you're in a place where you can't just go singing and dancing around the neighborhood, practice taking a few long, slow, full breaths as you focus on your body as it fills with air, then empties completely.

- Counter the desire to hold a drink in your hand by twirling a pencil between your fingers. The cognitive effort necessary to accomplish this feat will force your craving from your mind, at least temporarily. Besides, you're teaching yourself an interesting new skill!

Sleep

Most people who complete an alcohol fast report experiencing the best sleep they've had in years. Keep that in mind this week, because your sleep will likely be sporadic and disturbed. Give yourself the freedom to sleep when you feel tired, and don't berate yourself if you find yourself nodding off at odd times.

I'm about to tell you in the next section to stay away from coffee. However, if you're in a position where you *must* be awake and alert, it's more important to be kind to yourself. Drink some coffee now and sleep when you are able.

On the other hand, it is not uncommon to find yourself wide awake in the middle of the night. In this case, accept the current reality and find something to do that keeps your mind active and focused but not stressed. An idle mind is prime real estate for cravings, so head them off at the pass by reading, solving problems, fixing your car, or whatever you can do to keep your brain busy.

Diet

This week, your body is trying to rid itself of all the toxins that have built themselves up while you were drinking. It is working hard to return you to a state of normalcy. This is the time to be kind to yourself. Give yourself edible treats, while you also eat things that will help your body repair itself.

You may not feel very hungry this week. Or, you may feel ravenous. After all, alcohol prevents your body from using the nutrition you hand it, so you may be malnourished and not even know it. You don't need to eat huge meals to make up, however. It's better at this point to eat many small meals and snacks. Send your body a steady small stream of nourishment during these days. If your body craves a certain food, as long as it's not highly sugared, go ahead and enjoy it!

Drink plenty of water. As I mentioned back in the beginning of this book, alcohol tends to remove water from your body, so you may well be dehydrated when this week starts. Also, water will help to carry those alcohol-induced toxins out of your body. Now, don't go overboard; don't drink more than a quart in an hour's time. However, do keep up a steady stream of water, sipping throughout the day. If you get tired of plain old water, you can switch over to juice or a sports drink; just dilute these to reduce the sugar content. Because most alcoholic beverages contain sugar, you may also be withdrawing from a physical dependence on sugar. Just remember, your primary liquid should be water. Okay, you can squeeze in a little lemon for flavor if you want.

Especially this week, avoid coffee, sodas (especially diet sodas!), and dark tea. Herbal teas like chamomile, mint, and ginger can provide hydration and promote healing without the diuretic effects of their darker cousins. Again, drink these either entirely without sugar or with the smallest amount of honey you can tolerate. I would also recommend stevia as a natural source of sweetness; just avoid artificial sweeteners, as they will feed additional chemical toxins into your system.

Many of the dietary strategies I gave you for managing a hangover will apply to this week. Go back to Chapter 1 and review the section entitled "The Morning After."

Activities

Take a break from strenuous exercise this week, for the obvious reason that your body needs the time to heal and restore itself. Any serious exertion would take energy away from that task. This *doesn't* mean, however, that you should become a stand-in for The Blob! A casual walk, even a moderate hike, will help to stimulate your circulation and metabolism, as well as boosting your immune system. If you have a dog, some play time would be good for both of you. And if you can get out into the countryside, all the better.

Listen to your body and try to answer what it needs. If you feel like being with friends, go hang out with them at the mall or a restaurant. If you find yourself going stir-crazy, head out to the nearest arcade and pretend like you're a teenager. If you feel like being alone, get out into nature, browse your favorite craft shop or hardware store, or scrub your floors.

Support
If you haven't already, now's the time to rally some people around you for moral support. Take an inventory of the people in your life. Who can you count on to give you positive energy? Those are the people to spend time with this week. Go to lunch together, take a walk, sit around the kitchen table and chat, work together to wash and wax your cars, go to a museum, attend a concert. If you can't meet in person, talk over the phone or on Skype.

If you prefer a more formal setting, make a point of introducing yourself to an Alcoholics Anonymous group, or another support community. For additional suggestions, refer back to Chapters 6 and 7.

The Second Week – Beyond Detox
By this time, you should have developed some experience – if not finesse – at handling your **cravings**. They'll still be around, but you know how to deal with them and move on. If the struggle seems to be defeating you, this may be a time to seek out professional help. There's nothing wrong with bringing someone alongside to help bolster your resolve.

Sleep
Hopefully your body is allowing you to get a good night's sleep most of the time. If you haven't already established a **bedtime ritual**, this is the time to set one up. It will prime your mind and body to get the most out of your sleep. Refer back to Chapter 5 for additional information.

Spiritual

Alcohol is often used to fill a spiritual void, even if we are unaware of it. Whether religious or not, you have an inner part that is tuned toward things that transcend your mundane experiences of life. I suggest you give yourself time this week to evaluate your spiritual longings and needs and think about what you want to do to fulfill them.

Because of the connection between alcohol and spiritual awareness, this alcohol fast will affect your spirit. Change in spiritual focus inevitably leads to a change in the way we live.

Now's a good time for me to remind you to record in your journal what you're experiencing, discovering, and learning.

Change Your Thinking
In his book *Being Sober*, Harry Haroutunian, MD describes "Four Basic Shifts" that take place as we grow away from our involvement with alcohol. Because these adjustments are key to your growth going forward, I have summarized each shift below.

1. **"From Fear to Trust"** – We've already talked some about facing the fears that we hide from behind a bottle (or a can). We don't like exposing ourselves, especially our weaker selves. We don't like being vulnerable. But that's the only way to get past our fears.

   As you bring those fears out into the open, acknowledging them and owning them, you open up the door to change. It may feel at first as if the fear is getting even worse, but as you work through your fears and find ways to love yourself in the midst of them, you will grow in confidence that you can indeed face whatever life throws at you. When you notice this shift taking place, you can be confident that you are indeed growing.

2. **"From Self-Pity To Gratitude"** – When bad things happen to us, it is easy to sink into the posture of a victim. We can choose to submit to our situation and claim it as our reality, or we can acknowledge where we are now and

77

work to move forward through this difficulty. "This too shall pass" said a wise individual who obviously had found the door from self-pity to gratitude. There is always *something* to be gained from even the worst circumstances. That's the challenge, to find the good that is coming to you through your problems.

Instead of shrinking away from your painful circumstances, do the hard work of pressing into the situation, looking for the good, milking it for all the benefit you can get out of it. Instead of blaming others, pray for – and promote the good of - the people you feel like resenting.

This week, give yourself some time to do this short exercise: now that you are more aware of the effects of alcohol on your life, imagine yourself walking through a day in your life with each of these effects. Then imagine the same day, but this time you're free from all the effects of alcohol on your life. Walk through the day, fully aware of all the good you're experiencing. Let all these benefits feed your gratitude as you speak out loud each good thing you're glad to have.

3. **"From Resentment to Acceptance"** – The key to this transition comes when we realize that control is a myth. We try so hard to control our lives; we even try to control other people. But it's all futile. Might as well give up judging others and accept them as they are. That goes for ourselves, too. I'm a lot freer to live when I've abandoned the habit of judging myself for being human.

   According to Dr. Haroutunian, "acceptance is about giving up the need to control people or situations and understanding that, in reality, we never really had control to begin with." For me this has not come quickly; I couldn't just will it. The process of letting go has been a day by day – sometimes moment by moment – conscious practice that is still ongoing.

Let me suggest an exercise. The next time you find yourself feeling frustrated or angry because something – or someone – just isn't going "right", step back for a moment and look for what you are expecting. What are you afraid of? Yes, anger is often fear blown sideways, so if you can figure out why you're feeling angry or frustrated, you may well find something you're afraid of losing.

Own that fear. Embrace it. Give it the freedom to Be. This may well go against every fiber of your being, because in our culture it is taboo to show any sign of weakness. But only when you accept this part of you will you be able to address and heal the part that is hurting.

Look for the reality behind the fear. What is the worst that can happen? Sometimes our fears will start to look pretty puny when put up against the light of day. Even the worst catastrophe can be lived through, and probably has been survived, by someone, somewhere. Choose to trust that you, too, can survive this thing that you cannot control. Choose to trust that the Universe (or God) is for you, not against you, and that good will come of this. Yes, this third step builds upon the trust and gratitude you've already established.

4. **"From Dishonesty to Absolute Rigorous Honesty"** – At the heart of an alcohol fast is the willingness to stop hiding from ourselves. This may not make sense to you if you lack strong triggers that urge you to drink. Each trigger is an invitation to hide from some part of yourself. The process of looking behind the trigger to what is in me that I want to avoid, is the start of re-integrating my Self. This is the heart of "absolute rigorous honesty" or, as I prefer to call it, integrity.

Integrity goes beyond not lying to your customers and not cheating on your spouse. It has its roots in the concept of the integer. An integer is an indivisible whole, a thing that is the same through and through. No matter how you slice and dice it, you come up with the same substance.

Your month-long alcohol fast is an invitation to journey down the path of re-integrating the Self. Granted, this process will take much longer than thirty days, but by paying attention to your cravings and uprooting the fears at their source, you have a ready-made tool to help you begin to re-integrate the missing parts of yourself. You may well come out of this more fully human than before. And that's a good thing.

Diet

Continue to treat yourself to foods you like, but you may find you do not need to eat as much as last week. Now would be the time to start to shift your diet away from pre-packaged foods to fresh meat, fruits, and vegetables, whole grains, and healthy fats.

Continue to wean yourself off of any dependence on sugar. I suggest this week you keep track of everything sweet you eat or drink, other than fruit. If you find yourself eating more sugary snacks and drinking more soda than you think is healthy, you might consider finding a replacement. Fresh fruit, crunchy vegetables, even chips and dip can be a healthier alternative. When you need to sweeten something, try stevia or a touch of honey. I found grapes and nectarines to satisfy my sweet tooth and baby carrots, peppers or celery dipped in ranch dressing to stimulate my taste buds without too many calories.

Healthy Junk Food

Okay, that title may be a bit of a misnomer, but there are junk foods that are better than other junk foods, okay? Here are a few you can enjoy with minimal guilt:

- Graham crackers – Eat these instead of those high-sugar cookies.

- Sour cream – better than mayonnaise. I use it sometimes on sandwiches. I also learned from the Ukrainians to use a dollop to add flavor to soup.

- Dark chocolate – Now aren't you happy? I am.

- Pork rinds – they're much better for you than potato chips, and pretzels are better than both.

- Popcorn – All right, I suppose you need butter; just melt the real thing on it, and not too much. Also watch the salt and maybe add a little garlic powder or pepper for a change of flavor.

- Baby carrots, the little tiny ones. I know, it sounds like I'm trying to sneak something healthy onto the list, but these things are really good! They're sweet and crunchy...hmm, sounds a little like a pickle, but they satisfy the craving for something sweet and crunchy, don't they? There are days when you just need something to chew on.

- Coconut – Eat the unsweetened kind; it's high in calories so you don't need much, but it'll keep you from feeling hungry for a long time because of the fiber.

Smell And Taste
One thing people notice during this month of no alcohol is that they regain fresh awareness of smells and tastes. Feel free to enjoy the aromas and flavors around you. Play around with spices to give your food new flavors. Walk in a garden to smell the flowers. Light some aromatic candles. Experiment with essential oils. You might also want to play with aromatic shower gels or bath oils.

You can find aroma lights at any discount store. They usually fit in with your décor and look pretty. They plug right into an outlet and you put scented wax squares in them. The wax melts and disperses the scent in the room. The scents usually come in packets of six to nine squares, but you only need one. I save mine once they melt, because you can use them multiple times. I just take a knife and pop them out of the scent bowl and put them in a re-closeable plastic sandwich bag. The scent squares are very inexpensive.

Activity
Now is the time to re-introduce physical activity into your life. At the very least, take a short walk each day. If you have been accustomed to an exercise regimen, you can start up your program, after ratcheting the intensity back a few notches. Remember, your body has been rebuilding and restoring, so don't demand peak performance right off the bat. If you're a weightlifter, this week is a good time to go with lighter weights and increased repetitions. Save the heavy lifting for next week. Consider this a week for rebuilding and don't push yourself too hard.

Remember to play! Include pets, children, and friends in the merriment. Weather permitting, get outside and have some fun.

Third Week – Over The Halfway Mark
Yes, you've passed through the toughest part. Your cravings, while still present, are less of an issue. You're fairly experienced at handling them now; just don't be surprised if they crop up when you least expect them. Old habits sometimes die hard, but keep resisting. You've worked too hard to give in now.

Diet And Movement
Continue to fuel your body's restoration with fresh fruits and vegetables. Ensure that you get enough protein in your diet by eating meat, nuts, raisins, spinach, and dried apricots (for some strange reason, only the dried apricots are a significant source of protein). Keep on drinking plenty of water throughout the day.

Physical activity helps to distract you from cravings, and may even lessen them. Anything done outdoors has the added benefit of refreshing your breathing, enhancing your mood, and reinforcing your body's wake/sleep cycle.

Stages Of Change

A hallmark of Motivational Enhancement Therapy (MET), these stages of change, based on the Transtheoretical Model by Dr. Carlo C. DiClemente and Dr. James Prochaska, provide a useful roadmap to show you how far you have progressed in your thirty-day trek with no alcohol.

1. Precontemplation – This is before you were even aware. This stage often includes denial, e.g. "my drinking is not a problem." You may have completed this stage long before you picked up this book.

2. Contemplation – You are aware that your drinking has some negatives. This is when you do an informal risk/benefit analysis, asking yourself, "Is it worth the effort to give this up for 30 days?" This is pretty much what you accomplished by the time you reached Chapter 3.

3. Preparation/Determination – You're committed to making a change, now you're trying to figure out how to make it stick. That's when you learned about the 30-day no alcohol challenge and all the options you discovered in the past couple chapters.

4. Action/Willpower – This is when you take steps to implement your 30-day plan. You've been in this stage for going on three weeks now! Look back at all you've accomplished so far. You've walked through all sorts of difficulties and you're still staying the course! This calls for a celebration! Give yourself a special treat, run a victory lap, dance your victory dance, do a fist pump or whatever you do when you've just experienced a resounding success. You've earned it! Now the end is in sight. Prepare for even more fun next week.

5. Maintenance – This is what you'll be doing after your thirty days is up. But we'll talk more about that next week.

Fourth Week – Including The Final Two Days!

Diet And Activity
Continue to eat fresh foods as much as possible. The more you can avoid pre-processed foods, the more you will keep toxins out of your body in the first place. Keep on drinking plenty of water. And keep up your daily walks, playtime, and any exercise regimen you have committed to.

Boost Your Body
Here are some foods I suggest sneaking into your diet when you can, because they will help your liver function normally and will assist with its ongoing job of detoxifying your body and processing your food:

- Lemon/lime

- Pineapple

- Apples

- Walnuts (add a few to your breakfast cereal or eat them by themselves for a snack)

- Garlic (a little will help a lot.)

- Carrots

- Grapefruit

- Beets

- Cabbage

- Broccoli and cauliflower

- Turmeric (Sprinkle this spice on vegetable dishes or add to stew.)

- Spinach and other leafy green vegetables

- Avocados (yes, guacamole is a good thing!)

- Olive oil

- Green tea

Prepare To Celebrate

If you haven't decided how you want to celebrate the completion of thirty days of alcohol-free living, now's the time to start thinking. The day will be here sooner than you expect. However you choose to celebrate, make it something memorable!

And Then...

So, what are you going to do after your thirty days are up? Whether you've decided to continue your alcohol-free lifestyle or you decide to scale back your drinking, it's a good thing to devote some time this week to thinking out what you want your life to look like going forward. You've experimented with different ways of eating, drinking, exercising, and thinking about yourself. Even though you're well on the way to establishing some new habits, it's important to consciously choose which habits you intend to continue. Then you can make plans to ensure they don't get dropped in the shuffle of your ongoing life.

My life changed drastically after completing the fast. I decided not to drink alcohol at all, but I still cook with it, making sure all the alcohol cooks out before eating. I have a better relationship with my family and the friends that matter in my life. I weeded out all those old so-called friends who only wanted me for a good time while I was drinking. I replaced them with friends who share other interests with me like cooking, old movies, and music. I did better at my everyday job and was promoted.

While money is almost always a problem for most people, money became less of a problem for me because I wasn't spending several nights a week at the bar or purchasing expensive liquor to keep at home. I had more money to spend on the good things in life. I was able to concentrate better.

When you drink, it is like there is a yellowish film over everything you think and see. Life is fuzzy and unclear. Once you stop drinking and get through to a life of sobriety, that film lifts and the flowers in the front yard look more beautiful, they smell better, and you have the desire and strength to nurture them again.

Conclusion

You now have everything you need to successfully complete your own month-long abstinence from alcohol. You have a host of resources that can help you handle everything from drinking triggers to the social challenges that arise when you take a hiatus from drinking. I've given you the best strategies to handle cravings and stave off boredom. You also have at your disposal some wonderful healthy junk food ideas, along with alternative beverages to get you started. I have provided support resources, both natural and traditional, for surmounting any obstacles you face during the first month and coming years.

It isn't easy to stop drinking, even if you are a light drinker. Be sure you have committed to at least 30 days of abstinence so you can truly comprehend just how good you can feel without alcohol. The truly seductive, addictive, and deadly nature of alcohol has caused the early demise of many great men and women. So stay strong, and be sure to have a plan in place for those periods in time when you know you are going to be tempted. Have a strategy already in place to counteract the triggers you have.

I want you to know that if you do slip up in the process, it is possible to start over again and re-acquire the clarity of life you need. Do not be too hard on yourself. It's a difficult thing to stop drinking and live a life of sobriety, especially if you have been drinking for a long time. If you stumble, pick yourself up, dust yourself off, and begin your month-long abstinence challenge again. You have come so far already; just add to your arsenal of support, then use what you've already learned to complete the challenge successfully. Freedom from alcohol is well worth the effort.

After your month of abstinence, you may decide you can take a drink from time to time, but I hope you will be alert to the danger signs now. You have gained the skills to take evasive action, before you slip back into worshiping the bottle. You've learned them over the past 30 days, so don't hesitate to use them.

I'm very proud of you for taking the courage to accept this challenge. You are joining hands with the thousands who have gone before you, showing the entire world that, yes, it is possible to exchange old habits for better ones. You have made the decision; now take some action, burn your ships, get all alcohol out of the house and get your favorite strategies from this book in place so you can proceed forward to a brighter future.

You are on the brink of something great! You may well be standing where Bradley Cooper stood just a few years ago, realizing that he could either have alcohol or a successful life and career, but not both. You are now poised to follow him down the path where you will discover new truths about yourself, surprise yourself by your ability to live life to the fullest, and honor your capacity for sheer joy. You will find greater inner resilience than you thought possible. It's all waiting for you; you need only take the first step and keep moving forward and never give up until you have the health and joy that you deserve.

Thanks for reading.

I hope this book was able to help you to see yourself walking through the next thirty days, successfully mastering the No-Alcohol Challenge. The next step is to firm up that plan and start to live it out. Put a big star on today in your calendar, mark out thirty days from today and get busy living!

If this book helped you or someone you know then be sure to leave a nice review as soon as is convenient for you, it would be greatly appreciated. For more great knowledge of the world, be sure to check out my other books.

My Other Books

Be sure to check out my author page at:

USA: https://www.amazon.com/author/susanhollister

UK: http://amzn.to/2qiEzA9

Or simply type my name into the search bar: Susan Hollister

Thank You